SHRAPNEL WOUNDS

ALSO BY TOM CROWLEY

Featuring Matt Chance

Viper's Tail
Murder in the Slaughterhouse

Non-Fiction

Bangkok Pool Blues

TOM CROWLEY

SHRAPNEL WOUNDS

AN INFANTRY LIEUTENANT'S VIETNAM WAR MEMOIR

DOWN & OUT BOOKS

First Down & Out Books Edition October 2019

Down & Out Books
3959 Van Dyke Road, Suite 265
Lutz, FL 33558
DownAndOutBooks.com

Cover design: Tom Heffron
Cover art: *Landing Zone* by John O. Wehrle, CAT I, 1966. Courtesy of the National Museum of the United States Army

ISBN: 1-64396-090-3
ISBN-13: 978-1-64396-090-6

This book is dedicated to all my brothers-in-arms
who shared my war, and most especially
to those who didn't make it back home.
I owe all to them.

GLOSSARY

APC—Armored Personnel Carrier. Each division had at least one battalion that was equipped with these lightly armored tracked vehicles, which could carry a squad of soldiers inside. Each was armed with a .50-caliber heavy machine gun.

ARVN—Army of the Republic of Vietnam. The ARVN were our allies in the war against the communists. Rank could be purchased by wealthy Vietnamese who couldn't avoid service. The rank-and-file soldiers were often from poor farm families.

Bo doi—Literally "foot group." These were the rank-and-file North Vietnamese soldiers, who were often communist cadres. These were the troops who led the way into and occupied Saigon on April 30 1975, and came for Chi on May 1. The Viet Cong, the soldiers from the South, were relegated to a back seat for this show.

CAP—Combined Action Patrol. This was the core of the innovative pacification effort that joined U.S. Marine Corps volunteers with local regional force platoons in the I Corps area early in the war.

Charlie—The tag most often used by American troops to refer to the enemy, whether, Viet Cong or North Vietnamese Army. This came about as soldiers' slang from the phonetic designation of the words Victor (V) and Charlie (C) for Viet Cong.

CID—Criminal Investigation Division. This is the army's crime and special investigation unit. It grew out of a special military police unit stationed in Saigon during the war.

DOC—Death Other than Combat. This is the phrase the army used to account for soldiers who died in various accidents, truck crashes, chopper or plane crashes on routine flights, or drowning. Combat zones seem to accelerate the number of accidental deaths as troops become careless of dangers other than combat. The rate of such deaths was quite high, frequently up to 20 percent of in-country deaths per month in the years I cover in this book.

H&I—Harassment and Interdiction fire. A routine exercise of firing artillery into an area where no friendly troops were engaged with the enemy but in which there was intelligence or other reason to believe the enemy was moving. This was most often conducted at night when VC or NVA troops would be on the move to avoid American air power.

Hoc tap (***trại học tập cải tạo***)—Re-education camps operated by the communist government after the fall of Saigon. Hundreds of thousands of former South Vietnamese military officers and government workers were imprisoned without formal charges or trials. Thousands were tortured or abused, and some 165,000 people are believed to have died in the camps.

IED—Improvised Explosive Device. This is the current term for an explosive booby trap.

KIA—Killed in action.

LAW—Light Anti-tank Weapon. This was the first light hand-held shoulder-fired individual anti-tank weapon, a rocket in a narrow three-foot tube. It was deployed frequently in Vietnam to destroy VC bunkers at a distance.

L.T. (**ell-tee**)—The slang abbreviation for lieutenant often used by troops in a platoon when addressing a platoon leader they trust.

LZ—Landing zone. Most often used in discussing aerial assaults in the field.

Medicap—Medical Civic Action Program. This was a "hearts-and-minds" effort that basically involved a U.S. Army doctor, several medics, and a translator entering a village, holding a sick call, and treating all those who came for help. Sometimes efforts were made to gather intelligence or to persuade the villagers of the government's interest in their welfare.

MILPERCEN—Military Personnel Center (now called Perscom, or Personnel Command). The abbreviation was used for the army's military personnel command in Alexandria, Virginia. These are the gods of promotion for officers. This is where an officer's file of Officer Evaluation reports reposes and is brought out for study when it is promotion time each year and a promotion board is assembled. The real competition starts when the promotion step from captain to major arrives. Every officer waits to see if he will be "fast-tracked" promoted ahead of his peers.

NCO—Noncommissioned Officer. These are the career enlisted men with the stripes on their sleeves, grades E-5 (sergeant) through E-9 (sergeant-major). They often report to newly commissioned lieutenants officers but have the experience in daily matters that the army needs to keep things running. An issue in Vietnam, Iraq, and Afghanistan was that the NCOs were over-tasked and often ordered to do multiple tours after only short intervals at home in the U.S. This caused many to leave the service.

NLF—National Liberation Front. This was the Vietnamese political organization formed on December 20, 1960, to effect the overthrow of the South Vietnamese government and the reunification of North and South Vietnam. An overtly communist party was established in 1962 as a central component of the NLF, but both the military arm, the Viet Cong, and the political organization, the NLF, were said to include many non-communists. The NLF was represented by its own diplomatic staff in all communist countries and in several neutral ones. Students overseas paid attention to this organization as the political voice for the Viet Cong, but for American soldiers on the ground it was a non-factor. Charlie, the fighting force, was everything. History has shown us that, to the extent there were non-communists in the NLF, they were sheep marching with alligators, and at the end of the day it was well-fed alligators that emerged alone to claim victory.

NVA—North Vietnamese Army. These were the regular army troops from the North who were usually much better equipped, having artillery and tanks, than the Viet Cong or southern resistance troops.

OCS—Officer Candidate School. This is the course that provides the opportunity for enlisted men who are seen to have leadership potential to earn commissions as second lieutenants. At the time I attended, there were two OCS schools in the army, infantry and artillery, which were each six months long. The washout factor was usually 50 percent. Today the army has one OCS school for all branches, which is three months in duration.

OER—Officer's Evaluation Report. This is the powerful document, written by a continuing progression of superior officers after completion of assignments throughout a career, that ranks an officer in relation to his or her peers. The army has a method of taking these reports and evaluating whether an officer's performance is in the zone, meaning on a par with other officers of the same rank and length of service. Being promoted below the zone, ahead of one's peers is a very good thing; it means that you are fast-tracking and bodes well for your career and future promotion. Being above the zone at any point in your career means kiss your career goodbye. This is a career officer's matter of first concern.

PFC—Private First Class (E-3).

Punji Pits and Punji Stakes—Punji pits, four to six feet deep with a light covering of branches and leaves, were a common home-made Viet Cong method for injuring American troops. The stakes would be branches or bamboo, sharpened at both ends and set at the bottom of the pit in the hope the American soldier would tumble in and impale himself on the stakes.

Pup tent—Two shelter halves buttoned together, erected with poles and cords, and deployed to shelter two soldiers for a night.

R&R—Rest & Recreation. The label the military gives the one-week trips away from the battle zone. In Vietnam, it was usual for a soldier to have the opportunity once during his tour to get away to cities such as Bangkok, Singapore, Hong Kong, Tokyo, or even Honolulu.

RA—Regular Army. For both enlisted men and officers, "RA" denoted their permanent rank status, as opposed to reserve ranks, which could be temporary in nature. During the time of the Vietnam War, many enlisted men were drafted and their serial numbers started with "U.S.," which denoted a draftee. If the soldier reenlisted, he became RA.

ROTC—Reserve Officers' Training Corps. This is the college program that trains students in military matters as preparation for receiving a commission as a second lieutenant on active duty after graduation. Most major universities in the United States participate in the program.

RTO—Radio Telephone Operator. This is the soldier who carries the radio for the platoon leader, company commander, or battalion commander. This is a dangerous job because the enemy is looking for radios as a sign that the officer in charge is nearby.

S1 to S4—These are the designations for the staff positions that make the battalion or brigade function. All report to the battalion or brigade commander. S1 is the administrative job and the position is usually filled by a captain. S2 is the intelligence job, and the position is also usually filled by a captain. S3 is the operations, planning, and training job, and is usually filled by a major. This is a key job in the combat-arms promotion ladder. A rising officer should have experience in all the staff positions, but the operations job is key. S4 is the supply officer, and the position is usually filled by a captain.

Spec 4—Specialist 4th Class. This is the enlisted rank (E-4) just below the rank of sergeant with three stripes on his sleeve (E-5). This is equal in rank to a corporal.

Squad or Rifle Squad—The basic combat unit of ten men, which has been the building block for armies since the Roman legions. A typical rifle platoon such as mine fielded four squads plus the platoon sergeant, a medic, an RTO, and myself, forty-four soldiers in all. The reality was that we were never at full strength and operated with, at best, thirty-five men present for duty.

TOC—Tactical Operations Center. I use this phrase for our battalion operations center, but it can be used for any combat operations center of battalion size or larger. This is the combat communications and plans center wherein the daily operations of units are monitored.

USO—United Services Organization. A civilian organization that organizes recreation and support for the military members in the U.S. and overseas. Though not of the military, it works closely with the military establishment and has a presence on most bases and in many overseas activities.

Viet Cong or VC—This is a contraction of Viet Nam Cong-san (Vietnamese communist). This was the name most often given those fighting to overthrow the South Vietnamese government after 1956. As we went through airborne training during the war, when called to attention the troops responded with a hearty "Sat Cong"—Kill communists!

Viet Minh—An abbreviation of Việt Nam Độc Lập Đồng Minh Hội (League for the Independence of Vietnam). The Viet Minh was a communist national independence coalition formed on May 19, 1941, to seek independence from France. The Viet Minh opposed Japan during World War II, and then, respectively, France and the United States afterwards.

WIA—Wounded in Action.

WPPA—West Point Protective Association. This is the slang term used by enlisted men or non-West Point officers when they see preferential treatment being given to a West Point graduate by another West Point graduate. A good example is the failed effort made to help Lieutenant B enhance his evaluation report, which is cited in Chapter 12.

XO—Executive Officer. This is the officer reporting directly to the commander at the company, battalion, or brigade level who is responsible for taking the burden of administrative duties off the shoulders of the man who should be busy leading his troops in action. Lieutenant David, cited in Chapter 20, was the executive officer of Headquarters Company of the 4/9, and thus the man dispensing non-judicial punishment. His punishment of a soldier who was drunk on duty was the motivation for the soldier to attempt to kill him by fragging.

AUTHOR'S FOREWORD

I didn't want to write this book. But I did want to write the stories that are included in the book. I wrote them over a number of years, a decade or more, covering various episodes in my experience in Vietnam with war and with the young men (usually very young men) who fight wars.

After I wrote them I just left these vignettes on my computer, visiting them periodically, adding to them, broadening them. I found some of the stories very difficult to write. Over the many years that have passed, I don't recall ever relating them to anyone. I don't think I'm alone in that. I have many friends who are combat veterans, and I belong to the Veterans of Foreign Wars in the United States, an organization solely for those who have served in one of America's many overseas military ventures. Never have I heard another combat veteran go into a detailed description of his experiences, even during occasional evenings filled with drink.

It has seemed to me that books on war fall into one of several categories. There are the autobiographical books by authentic war heroes. Post-World War II books such as *To Hell and Back* by Audie Murphy and *Those Devils in Baggy Pants* by Ross S. Carter are good examples of what thrilled me as a teenager. Of course, these men were superheroes, and their experiences were not necessarily representative of the lives of the common soldier, but I found them very inspirational and still do.

Then there are the war-correspondent books, some of which were very well written. Some, such as Michael Herr's Vietnam book *Dispatches*, gained notoriety as much for the drug-fueled antics of the writer and his colleagues as for the coverage of the fighting man. The problem with books in this category is that they have nothing to do with the daily reality of war most soldiers experience. *Dispatches* hops from one of the correspondent's adrenaline highs to another, as if that was the norm. As well-written as it is, and however wonderful for exposing the hypocrisy of the American military leadership, it is more reflective of peaks of action, such as Khe Sanh, and skips over the troughs of a soldier's life in between. Also, much of the book is filled with the correspondent's lifestyle issues in the rear, as he returns to Saigon to join other correspondents in their self-admiration society. Certainly in Vietnam, and increasingly elsewhere today, many reporters seem to follow this trend and report on the reporting, as if that is part of the war. This did not reflect to me the reality of Vietnam in any sense, though I can understand the attraction of reporting only the crashes at car races. Definitely, the peaks of combat are part of a grunt's life, and Vietnam had more than enough crashes for journalists to report.

I give a lot of credit to the attempt made in *War* by Sebastian Junger, a professional writer who, along with photo-journalist Tim Hetherington, went to great effort to document the daily existence of a platoon of combat soldiers from the 173rd Airborne Brigade in Afghanistan over the course of a year. Nevertheless, reporters are visitors, even if more frequent and longer staying then most. Much of the reporting reverts to the theme of how good we reporters are for doing this. Yes, well done, reporters, but it's the wreckage of combat and of combatants with serious issues before and after their service that receives the attention. The truth is that most grunts suffer and cope quietly with their pain both during their service and afterwards. That is not the stuff of headlines. And, always, there is the issue that the very presence of reporters and cameras elicits precisely the activity and dialogue the reporters are looking for. Some guys just want to be on camera.

When finally determining whether to embark on this project, I decided my goal would be to do as much as possible to stick to the reality of the common soldier. I want to show the effect on those bearing the brunt of the war, of the failure of military leadership at higher levels, of the reality of avoidable non-combat deaths, and of the costs of the careerist approach taken as a matter of course at the expense of the non-career young men whom leaders use as their tools of war.

Few of the millions of combat veterans really speak out. Several things moved me to take on this task, as much an emotional as a literary challenge. The first was that I had already taken up writing and my first publication, the non-fictional *Bangkok Pool Blues*, was followed by two novels, *Viper's Tail* and *Murder in the Slaughterhouse*. In those books, spurred on by my editor, I shared some of the realities of my combat experiences through the character of my protagonist. While speaking on the book promotion trail, I found that audiences were just as interested in hearing the stories I hadn't shared in my books as the few that I had. They invariably gave me a warm and interested reception, and on each occasion they strongly encouraged me to write more about my combat experiences. I found this reaction to be unsettling. I felt, as I told each audience, that I was not emotionally strong enough to write these stories. The process of writing forced me to revisit painful memories, again and again, to reopen old wounds I had covered up for years.

For a while, months and then years, those memories lay dormant. The thought of completing and publishing my stories had been planted, but the will still wasn't there. The fear of the high emotional cost involved in re-engaging with my writing, which at times prompted suicidal thoughts, was too great. Then one night I had dinner with a Thai friend, an editor; his adult son, who is a professional cinematographer; and three British visitors to Bangkok. My friend, by way of introducing me, cited my books and my experiences in combat in Vietnam. Normally, these things are acknowledged and conversation moves on to the activities of others present and their interests. On this night, it did also, until later in the evening. Then, over the second pint of Killian's ale, my friend brought up the experiences of his Irish father-in-law in the Royal Navy in the North Atlantic in World War II. This man had the incredible experience of serving on three different ships that were all torpedoed and sunk by German U-boats. My friend's point was that on only one occasion, late in his life, on a quiet night, while sharing a drink at home, did his father-in-law bring up his experiences along with some of the details. The other men at the table that night then joined in. All of them had relatives, mostly grandfathers, who had served in the British military in World War II. They all said that, with one or two exceptions, the old men had never spoken about the hardships and losses they had experienced. I mentioned that I understood, that as a Vietnam veteran and a writer I had put a number of my stories on my computer but had left them there. I doubted I would ever do anything more with them. Then my friend pushed me to share with the group one of my experiences.

That experience is described in the chapter in this book entitled "Riding Home with the Guys." The reaction of the group was unanimous and strong: "You've got to write these stories. They should be told."

As I write this, it is well over a year since that dinner. First, I had to honor some other writing obligations. In truth, I used these as a continuing excuse not to take on the challenge of writing about my war. Two significant things have happened since. First, my writing desk is clear. Second, I had the opportunity to meet a veteran of the war in Iraq, Captain Pearl Phaovisaid, a young Thai-American woman who served in the U.S. Army as a Blackhawk helicopter pilot with fifteen months duty in Iraq. I felt such a strong bond with this youthful veteran, who shared many of my reactions to war and the military, I decided that it was time to tell my stories.

I'm involved in them for the most part, but they are not meant to be about me. I was not a hero. The reality is that I was just a 'grunt', as the military people say. In the army or marines, that is just a guy carrying a rifle in the jungle or the field. I was a soldier with no special tabs or berets, nor any claim to expertise in killing. One will not find here the epic suffering and heroism of World War II's Battle of the Bulge. Neither are there the days of courage and insanity of Vietnam's Hamburger Hill, an unnecessary battle that our ambitious generals inflicted on their troops. Rather, the stories here merely represent the everyday circumstances confronting the young men and women we send to fight the overseas battles our political leaders feel inspired to take on. I have come to believe that these accounts represent experiences shared by combat veterans in every army that has ever taken the field, from the days of Alexander the Great until now. Weapons and tactics may change with time, but realities for the grunts at the bottom of the pile, doing the actual fighting, never change. The wounds they carry home, physical and otherwise, are the same.

I believe combat veterans will connect with these stories. I hope their families and the general public will too.

September 1966

The number of American military:

Killed in action (KIA) was 313

Wounded in action (WIA) was 2,652

Non-combat deaths (DOC) was 85

CHAPTER 1
FIRST LESSON

The jungle is an oppressive force. *National Geographic* would have us believe that it is continuously creating new life, but the opposite is equally true. The jungle is constantly dying and rotting. We could smell it in the humid, sweltering air; we could feel its corruption on our sweat-soaked skin as we slowly made our way along the footpath.

I had expected a change of atmosphere when we closed on the abandoned village, but not such a fetid change. The huts, with their mud floors, rotting bamboo walls, and collapsing thatched straw roofs, were clearly long abandoned, yet they still retained the stench of putrefaction.

The village lay at the intersection of a river and a large canal. A smaller canal ran through it, bordered by twin footpaths where the huts were clustered. There was little room between this waterway and the wetland and bamboo growth at the edge of the forest, which pressed right up against the huts. The village lay dank and dark as the shadows of the approaching night loomed over us.

I was told to call in the squad from my platoon that had been left on the stay-behind ambush. They came in about twenty minutes later and joined the troops who lay along both sides of the two footpaths that traversed the village.

When we arrived there was only a single hut left unoccupied, the one nearest to the thick stand of bamboo separating the village from the forest. I entered and saw that there was no furniture apart from a couple of wooden stools and a rough wooden platform three feet off the ground, which a Westerner might take for a dining table but which served as a bed. I sat down on the bed, dropped my backpack, and told my radio-telephone operator (RTO) to put his equipment on it to make sure it would stay dry. I was satisfied as I looked around that at least we wouldn't be sleeping in the mud that night.

Having taken that short break, I knew I had to see to the placement of my platoon and find out if we had any specific orders for the night. I left the hut and found Sergeant Amado on one knee alongside the footpath, checking on how the platoon was arranged. He told me the stay-behind squad was back inside the company perimeter. I had just started to talk to him about how best to cover the way we had come in when it started.

We received a burst of automatic weapons and small-arms fire, not from the direction of our entry route, but very close by, on the other side of the bamboo growth behind the adjacent huts. For me, it was the first time under fire, and I had the silly thought that "it's just like they say," with the sound of the bullets whizzing past your head like a bee flying by at high speed. In as much as I was already bent down on one knee and leaning over to speak with Sergeant Amado, it was easy for me to hit the ground. Of course, at first, we weren't sure of the direction of fire, so the troops opened up in response pretty much along the way we had come in, but off to the side a bit.

After about three minutes, the incoming firing stopped and we received orders to cease fire. I checked with the squad leaders to see if we had casualties and found that no one had been hit. I was told to send a squad back up the trail, to open fire and push towards where we thought the enemy fire had come from. I did so, but there was no response. The Viet Cong had either followed us and gone to the jungle-covered side of the village to take us under fire or, as I later came to think was more probable, had anticipated where we were going and waited on the other side of the bamboo for all our troops to place themselves in their village, and then opened up. After they had fired off a magazine or two they took off.

All the reconnaissance had finished and we were set for the night, having put a listening post in place fifty meters outside the perimeter. I walked back into the hut and got my second major shock of the day following my introduction to enemy fire and the abrupt possibility of death it had presented. The bamboo wall of the hut, right behind the wooden platform I had been sitting on for a minute or two, had a long string of holes running left to right about a foot above the platform's level. If I had remained sitting there instead of kneeling out on the trail in front of the hut, at least two of those rounds would have pierced my chest. Of course, the VC were out to kill as many Americans as possible, not just me. It was just chance that I had sat there in the hut, talking to my RTO for a few seconds while the VC were on the other side of the bamboo thicket. I was sure they had heard our voices so, when they opened fire, that had seemed like a good direction in which to shoot. For me it was just like the movies. It could have been Rambo with the line of machine gun bullets stitched along the wall. Only this was real, and it was a wall I had been sitting against. It hit me later that the reason we had escaped injury was very simple. The VC who had shot at us, maybe only five or six men with a couple of AK-47s, had been standing up, unable to see through the bamboo, so they would have held their weapons above waist-height, tight and close to their chests to steady the automatic fire. As a result, the rounds went high as the American soldiers had all laid or sat down on the ground after hours of tough, hot walking through thick brush. The bullets went over our heads. Nevertheless, I now clearly understood the message. They. Had. Meant. To. Kill. Me. It left an impression. That was my first lesson. Now I understood what war was all about for the guys on the ground: It's about killing. Killing and surviving. Nothing else.

CHAPTER 2
LEARNING DAYS

In my pre-teen years, through my reading, I found the idea of being in the military and engaging in military combat attractive. I was a prodigious reader and, with the local public library on the same block as my home, I had a ready source of books. I had started to explore the library a few years earlier with guidance from the friendly librarian, who led me to the class of American books by Mark Twain, James Fenimore Cooper, and Herman Melville. The most outstanding warrior amongst the characters, Hawkeye, captured my imagination and led to my further exploration of books concerning American heroes of World War II. I scored at the top in a general intelligence test in school and I remember an eight grade teacher, a nun at my Catholic primary school, asking what I was reading at home. I brought a book to school for her to see and it shocked her a bit. That book was *Those Devils in Baggy Pants,* the story of Ross Carter and his combat experiences with the 82nd Airborne Division from Sicily to the Battle of the Bulge and on to Germany in World War II. Other books, such as Audie Murphy's *To Hell and Back,* followed, and somehow at that time the idea formed within me that I would one day be involved in similar combat roles as an airborne soldier.

I remember one year at the Wisconsin State Fair, inside the

one-mile oval race track, that the army put on a demonstration of the rifle platoon in the attack, complete with smoke grenades and shooting off lots of blank ammo rounds. They attacked a supposed enemy machine gun nest in the middle of the oval and showed the fire-and-maneuver tactics the platoon was supposed to use. They had some fake casualties and showed the medics coming to carry the wounded off the field in stretchers. I thought it was impressive, but I couldn't help wondering if it was really all that simple.

My initial battle was just to make it through my teen years. I started working at twelve with a fairly large paper route, more than one hundred customers, for the *Milwaukee Journal.* We were a family of seven children and definitely poor due to my dad's alcohol problems and lack of work motivation. Half of my weekly take of $25 from the paper route went to my mom to help out at home. Working after school conflicted with my ability to participate in school football and baseball, and fomented an anger, the early realization that life's not fair, that many kids from poor families come to when they look around and see other kids not having to fight the basic survival fight they are waging. A growing chip on my shoulder was made much worse when my five-foot-tall mom, with whom I was very close, and who literally had physically fought for her kids, died after a long illness, of a heart attack, on my fifteenth birthday. My life at school just went into a downward spiral after that. At first, I was able to take off of work and participate successfully as a halfback on the football team, but then the need for money had me back at work at a variety of jobs as soon as I turned sixteen. My grades, which had been in the A and B range in primary school, plummeted to C's and D's—and some failures—as I simply could not cope with my anger and focus on my studies. It culminated in my not being eligible for sports at all and then, a real shock to me, not being able to graduate with my high school class. I remember being with my friends from the football team during that graduation period as we went drinking. (Milwaukee is a beer town, after all.) I was so angry at the world I picked a fight with a good friend, a guard on the football team who didn't want to fight back, and forced him into a haymaker-throwing contest. Fortunately neither of us had much of a haymaker. After collecting a few bruises and with my temper cooled, we called it off. That fight was one of a long series of fights I had picked over the years, going back to fourth grade. The anger and resentment had grown over the years, but the chip on my shoulder was there from early on.

My failure to graduate was the shock I needed to shake off my self-pity and get on with life. I was still angry at the world, but I saw that if no one was there to help, I had to get my act together and help myself. I couldn't take my dad's drinking and weaknesses anymore, so I argued it out with him and left home during my senior year. Thankfully, an older sister was there to take me in to live with her and her family. I kept working part time, graduated a semester late, and signed up for community college, which was all I could afford. The Draft was then active and all eighteen year olds had to register. I had registered for the Draft as a college student, so I was deferred. That was until the spring of my first year, when I was in a car accident, hit from behind by a driver going too fast on a foggy night. I was forced to drop out of school. Then I learned that I was very probably going to be drafted in the coming year. I didn't like the probably part. I went on down to the army recruiting office in town and asked directly what time frame I had, whether I would be back in school or in the army. This was early 1964, and while the army wanted young bodies, it wasn't feeling the pressure it would in a few more years. The noncommissioned officer I spoke with let me know that the Draft would get me before the end of the year, but if I wanted to volunteer I could pick the date I would go into the service and the GI Bill would be there to help me finish school afterwards. Like a lot of low-income kids, I decided to accept the deal. I decided to work through the summer and enjoy it as much as I could and to go into the army after Labor Day. Thus, in September 1964, I reported to Union Station in Milwaukee to catch the first train ride I had ever taken and start down the trail to basic training at Fort Leonard Wood, Missouri.

CHAPTER 3
PREPARATION FOR WAR

Much of the process of arriving in the military had been forced on me, beginning with the lack of money to continue school, but there was one part of the process that I understood was up to me. As I thought it over in the months leading to my enlistment, I saw that part as the most important, my attitude. It has been said that attitude is everything, and I believe that is true. Prior to getting on that train to Fort Leonard Wood, I had made up my mind that I was going to be the best at everything I was introduced to and that I was going to volunteer for everything that I could. The army could dictate the process, but I was going to drive things with my response. I thought this was the only way to go, so I was surprised to find a good number of young guys on that train, some whom I knew from primary school, felt that they would keep the lowest profile possible and just go along. They saw military service as a burden to be eased through with as little work and exposure as possible. I saw military service as an opportunity to be seized. There was nothing they would throw at me that I couldn't take. There was nothing they could tell me to do that I couldn't handle. That was the best decision I ever made. That attitude, plus the still very large chip on my shoulder, would pay dividends over the next four years.

I found basic training to be remarkably easy and, in many

instances, fun. For anyone who had participated in school sports, especially the twice-a-day August football practices in full pads with the sun blazing down and the coaches yelling at you constantly and practicing water discipline, the harassment of the drill instructors (DIs) and their call to "give me twenty" push-ups was just a familiar par-for-the-course activity. The early morning runs singing Jodie chants came to be a fun routine.

The DIs quickly selected several recruits to be acting corporals and acting platoon sergeants to enforce order in the barracks when they were not present. I was picked as an acting platoon sergeant, which led to my first fist-throwing incident in the military.

One day midway through the eight-week course an acting squad leader from another platoon who had become a casual friend of mine came to me to complain. He said he had ordered one of his squad members to take out the trash at the end of the night and the guy had refused. I asked him what he had done. He said he had gone to the acting platoon leader, and the platoon leader told him to drop it. The acting squad leader said it was a major problem for him as the squad were just laughing at him now. Don't ask me why, but I decided to handle it for him. I told him to get the same guy to bring out the trash that night at 9:30, and he agreed.

I was waiting in the dark by the trash bins when the guy came out and my first thought was, thank God he's my size as I really hadn't an idea how big the guy might be. I was 5 feet, 10 inches tall and about 170 pounds. This guy was the same. I didn't waste any time. I just asked him if he was the asshole who had refused his squad leader's order the previous night. He said, "Yeah, so what?" I said, "So this," and started throwing punches. This guy turned out to be tough. The two of us must have spent twenty minutes trying to put each other down. If you've ever been in a real fist-throwing match, you'll realize that twenty minutes is an eternity. Finally, I realized that this could go on all night. We were just too well matched, and neither of us had a knock-down punch.

Finally I called it and said, "Enough!" and told him to go back to the barracks and just follow orders. He said okay, and that was it.

Or I thought that was it. I hadn't understood how word gets around. He told his acting platoon leader, who came to me the next day and said he would report me for beating up one of his guys. I told his acting platoon leader to fuck off, that I was just doing the job he should have been doing. The bottom line was that a complaint was lodged and the DI talked to me. I don't remember the words of admonishment, but I do remember that he was really pleased with what I had done. He loved it. It's what he and the other DIs would have liked to be able to do with those who recruits who weren't responsive to orders, but the army wouldn't allow them to do so.

Another part of that incident was that the guy I had the fight with, showed his respect for me several times after that, and I did for him. He was a tough kid. If we had served together after that, we could have been buddies. I always wondered what happened to him in the years after in his military journey.

About the sixth week of the cycle, I was taken out of ranks and sent over to an old wooden barracks left over from World War II. It had a sign on it stating it was the testing and evaluation center. I had been selected to take what was essentially an IQ test. As I went to enter the building and go up the back stairs to the second floor, an NCO (noncommissioned officer) passed me and vaulted up the stairs, two at a time. I noticed that he was wearing a green beret, which signified he was a Special Forces soldier. In those days, this was the army's only special unit and he was the first of these guys I had seen. I was impressed at the sheer physical energy this man manifested, and I thought, maybe, some day down the road, I might go that path. Even though my grades in school had been mixed, I have always been able to test well.

A week after that test the training company commander called me in. He told me I had pretty well maxed the test, scoring 157 points. I had, and have now, no frame of reference for that, but I understood he meant it was good. I didn't know what to say, so I just said, "Yes, sir." He explained that, along with my good record in basic training, I was eligible to apply for Officers' Candidate School (OCS) and the opportunity for a commission. He said it could be a year or more away and it would mean going on into further training in the infantry and becoming an infantryman, whether I succeeded in getting into and passing through OCS or not. He had a simple question, "Do you want to apply?" Of course my answer was "Yes, sir." I had made my mind to go all the way, and this was the next logical step.

As it came time for Basic Training graduation, I understood I was a candidate for Outstanding Trainee of that cycle. It was a close contest with several candidates. There was a grade for physical training, one for an obstacle course contest, a leadership evaluation, and a grade for training achievements, primarily the shooting scores we had posted with the M-14 rifle. My DI, who was pushing for me to get the award, told me he was very disappointed that I had come in second in the overall evaluation. He thought I deserved the award. I was second in the physical testing and first in leadership, but my score in shooting was just Sharpshooter, and that was on my second try. I had never handled a weapon before. The guy that was selected had scored an Expert badge. So be it. I made up my mind that I was going to be first in the next course of Advanced Infantry Training (AIT) at Fort Jackson, South Carolina.

CHAPTER 4
INFANTRY TRAINING

Getting to Fort Jackson entailed another series of train rides, only now it was mid-November and the weather was very cold and wet. I was exhausted after basic training ended and had gotten very sick with a fever and some type of flu. The army had issued me a heavy winter coat, which extended below my knees, and I wrapped myself in it and just slumped in the seat. The train trip took more than twenty-four hours, including extended stops along the way. I was one miserable soldier.

It was a bit warmer when I arrived at Fort Jackson and gathered on the first day with the group of trainees that would be accompanying me through the eight-week advanced infantry course. Fort Jackson was a rather rundown old base and a comedown from Fort Leonard Wood. Wood was primarily an engineering post and had modern brick barracks for the trainees, with separate squad rooms, adequate heating, and decent toilets and showers. Much of Fort Jackson was still using wooden barracks and buildings left over from World War II. All were set up about two feet off the ground on concrete blocks. We had a coal-fired stove in the open barracks with twenty guys in double bunks up and down one side and twenty guys up and down the other, open toilets at one end along with group showers that put out cold water as often as not. My immediate impression was that this was not going to be fun.

There were several other changes that quickly became apparent. I was not one of those selected to be an acting NCO. Those assignments had already been decided by the time I got to my new unit. I was going to be just one of the guys, which was a relief in some ways but meant that I would be pulling my share of kitchen police (KP) duty: peeling potatoes, cleaning the grease traps and stove tops after cooking was over, along with garbage toting and floor washing duty in addition to my training chores. KP in any unit is no fun, but it's a special pain in the ass in training units as the cooks love to pile their special brand of abuse on the trainees.

I noted a real shift in the background of the guys going through training. The basic training group at Leonard Wood was comprised of about 25-percent college grads, 25-percent of guys who had some college but for one reason or another had stepped back from school for a period of time as I had and drawn Uncle Sam's attention, and the rest were almost all high school grads. The average age was around twenty-one. At Fort Jackson I got the definite impression that the college grads had for the most part gone to other military occupational specialties (MOS in military nomenclature) than the infantry, such as intelligence, administration, and engineering. We were all about the same age group, but the average education had gone down markedly. Also, a lot of the guys in my training company were from the East Coast, a louder and tougher-talking group then the Midwest guys I was used to.

So I was just one of the guys; I would be just another trainee. That was okay. The training NCOs knew that I was an applicant for OCS and they would be watching me closely. I made up my mind that I would be the best soldier I could be throughout training and look for opportunities to stand out.

In general, this course was much tougher than basic training. Besides the much rougher living conditions, the PT exercises were tougher, the runs were longer, and the hikes tougher with more equipment to carry. We also spent a lot more time in the field, including a lot of cold, rainy nights in pup tents. We got some map and compass work (land navigation, as the military called it). This was a first for me. I liked it and took to it right way.

Also, we expanded our weapons training. I got to throw my first hand grenade, which gets your attention as you understand that once the pin is pulled there is no going back. We qualified with the M-14 rifle and once again, to my chagrin, the best I could do was Sharpshooter, a step down from Expert. We got to qualify with the M-14 E-2, the version of the M-14 that had a switch to turn it to automatic fire. The qualification with the automatic rifle was walking down a range with pop-up targets coming up left and right fifty to seventy-five meters ahead of you as you progressed. We had a twenty-round magazine in the rifle, which we were expected to change once as we walked along shooting down the targets. This was great fun. I loved it.

I learned one very important basic of automatic weapons fire from range instructors. Don't miss high. The bullets are wasted. If you're going to miss, miss low, because the bullets can still ricochet and hit the target. The importance of controlling the rise of the weapon as it fires was stressed along with the need to limit the automatic fire to short bursts.

We also got to fire the M-60 machine gun, which fired the same 7.62mm round as the M-14. The M-60 was also great fun, and all the same principals applied: fire short bursts. The mantra said "fire a burst of six" as you held the trigger down. This was based on what the military termed the cyclic rate of fire of the weapon. Again, it was stressed to shoot low and let the rounds ricochet or climb to the target. I thought it was all excellent training.

About six weeks into the course, I got the chance I was looking for to separate myself from the crowd. I had been comfortable with all the training and had done well, but I didn't know how I stood with the training NCOs. Although they were still distant, they had become friendlier as the course went on. Then I was selected along with ten other guys to serve sentry duty over a weekend. This is a boring, role-playing routine in which the trainees selected would carry unloaded M-14s and walk up and down in two-hour shifts, "guarding" some selected buildings on the base. This was done no matter what the weather was like, and rain was a real companion in the South Carolina winter. All the trainees were to wear fresh, neatly pressed uniforms, spit-shined boots, and white gloves to look their military best as they did their shifts. To encourage the trainees to do their best to meet the requirements, it was the practice that one trainee would be selected from the ten, through inspection. The inspection included having your rifle inspected for cleanliness, using your rifle properly to "present arms," and a quiz about the passwords and orders of the day.

The trainee selected as the best of those inspected would serve as "Colonel's Orderly," in which case the trainee would get a letter of commendation and be allowed to spend the guard shift indoors assisting with the supervision of the other guards. I worked hard on my rifle and uniform, especially my boots, on which you could see your face reflected if you looked closely. Handling my rifle and memorizing and quoting back the required information was no problem. I got picked as the "Colonel's Orderly" for that weekend.

One of the other guys pulling guard duty that weekend who was hoping to get selected told me that, "As soon as you walked in, I knew you had it." A bonus I hadn't known about was that a letter over the colonel's signature was sent to my family noting the selection. That was nice. I had not been writing home a lot, and my older sister said it was good of the colonel to write for me.

The day before the graduation ceremony, I found out that I was being considered for trainee of the cycle again, and I was one of two final candidates the DIs were evaluating. I was told to report to the company commander's office, where I and the other candidate would be quizzed on our knowledge of military matters, which included the chain of command and questions about weapons and map and compass work. I was dismayed to find out the guy I was up against was twenty-four years old and had enlisted in the army after service in the Marine Corps, where he had been an E-5—a buck sergeant, wearing three stripes. Sad to say, I came in second again. I remember the question he got right and I was unsure of had to do with the meaning of the use of certain colors in map reading. Second place was getting old, but I went away pretty comfortable. It was clear the training NCOs were comfortable with me as an OCS candidate, though I still had to make it past the interview phase, which was months in the future. The staff wished me well.

CHAPTER 5
FORT JACKSON: PERMANENT PARTY

After graduation from AIT, I was given orders assigning me as what was termed "permanent party," working with the infantry training battalion at Fort Jackson. Also, I was promoted from E-1, which was the lowest rank, the one newly inducted trainees were given. My pay as an E-1 had been $65 a month. I believe as an E-2 that I was boosted up to $78 a month. I was still what the NCOs called "slick sleeves" because I had no stripes on my sleeves. That would have to wait until I was promoted to E-3 or private first class in a couple of more months and would be authorized to wear a single stripe on each sleeve.

The Fort Jackson assignment was to be my duty assignment until I passed or failed the oral examination for OCS, which I was told would be a couple of months down the road. In the meantime, the captain commanding headquarters company of the training battalion told me to "keep your nose clean"—not to get into trouble with the NCOs and enlisted staff residing in the company barracks and those responsible for running the various training ranges on which I would be assisting.

At first, I didn't understand what the captain was warning me about. After four months as a trainee, even the simple barracks life improvements seemed a real step up to me. Just to have a single bed, not a bunk bed, and shower stalls with hot water made me feel as if I had arrived.

I soon learned what the problems could be. All military organizations, I am sure, have a major alcohol problem. I wasn't averse to having a beer, but these guys were major drinkers when they were off duty, and a few were sipping while on duty. They wanted me to drink with them at their pace. I became a target when they learned that the reason I was kept at Fort. Jackson was that I was potentially going on to OCS if I passed the oral exam. The mean streak came out in some of the NCOs, and especially in one rough-looking guy who was an E-4, a Specialist 4th Class. He was a very tall redneck from rural South Carolina and was determined to make it tough for the Yankee who thought he was going to be an officer. He started by posing as a friend, which surprised me, but I soon saw he wanted to drag me along to situations in which I could be forced to drink a lot and get into the trouble the captain had warned me against. I soon cut him off, but the result was that he and the other NCOs in the barracks arranged to basically have me shunned. Barracks life is always boring, but with no one to talk to in my barracks, it became a prison. My weekends were horrible, and escaping into Columbia, the university town the post was next to, was no answer as the town was divided into the college kids at the university, whom I might identify with but who in no way could identify with an enlisted soldier from the post, and the townies my age who might have finished high school but also had no interest in mixing with soldiers from out of town. Weekend life was arid.

Thankfully, my weekdays kept me really busy and gave me a window into how the army training world worked. I rotated assignments, assisting on a number of ranges that provided infantry training such as camouflage, fire and movement for rifle squads, and the hand grenade range. I found the NCOs running these courses much more receptive to me. Several of them wore the Combat Infantry Badge (CIB), a coveted award composed of a miniature silver Revolutionary War-style long rifle against a blue background and a silver wreath that was awarded to those who had served extended time—at least three months—in combat. Most of these NCOs had served in the Korean War and were in their thirties. When these guys talked about combat and life in a combat zone, usually only in indirect ways, you *had* to listen. We had one older, forty-plus, pot-bellied NCO who looked like a slovenly wreck due to his drinking, but everybody treated him with respect. He had served in World War II and had parachuted into Holland with the 82nd Airborne Division. He was friendly and a nice guy, but he just couldn't beat the drink. He was an E-6, staff sergeant, three stripes up and one down, but at his age and with his record he should have been at least an E-8, a first sergeant or master sergeant with three stripes up and three stripes down. My understanding is that he kept getting busted for getting drunk and missing duty. Only the army would put up with him, but everybody seemed to think that was a fair deal.

All of the training ranges were located in a large area of scrub pine forests around the base headquarters, down several miles of narrow macadam roads or, eventually, dirt roads. The soil in the area is a very poor sandy mix. I hadn't been doing any physical workouts since my graduation from AIT and assignment to the permanent unit, but it hit me after a couple of weeks that I couldn't allow my conditioning to deteriorate. Usually there was a truck at the headquarters building that would take the training staff out the five or six miles to the ranges early in the morning, around 8:00 a.m., to open up the facilities and prepare for the day's training. I decided to stop taking the truck and instead ran out to the range in my boots and fatigue work uniform starting at 7:00 a.m. every work-day morning. It was quite difficult, especially when the hardtop ended and I had to run on the sandy surface. In the beginning, I discovered that I couldn't run the entire distance; I was reduced to running and walking. But that was okay. I just kept at it. Sometimes NCOs driving their own cars came along and offered me a ride, but I always declined and explained that I needed the workout.

My determination in this soon earned the respect of the NCOs I worked with, and I could feel that, unlike the guys in the barracks, they were moving to on my side and cheering me on in my efforts. Gathered around the wood stove in the range huts early in the cold mornings, drinking acidic black coffee, they started telling me how to be a good officer, understand the enlisted point of view, and have the guts to resist stupid orders from above. They universally bad-mouthed West Point officers, said the West Pointers had no interest in taking care of the men but are "just putting in time until they get their battalion commander's position." This encouragement meant a lot to me. It in some ways helped me answer the question I had been struggling with, which was "Why in hell did I think I'm qualified to be an officer?" They told me that one part of the answer was that I could bring an understanding of what it was like to be in the ranks and devote myself to accomplishing the mission and taking care of my men at the same time. I could see the value in what I was bringing to the position with that frame of mine.

In March I was notified that I was to a put on a fresh uniform, "breaking starch" as the army calls it. Literally meaning to push open the legs and arms of a uniform that had been cleaned and heavily starched to get that sharply pressed look the military prizes in garrison. I was to appear before the officers who would interview me to determine my worthiness to attend OCS. I remember almost nothing of that interview with a major and a captain, except that they weren't looking for world knowledge on my part but seemed to be searching for commonsense answers. Having no ideas was unacceptable, but qualifying an answer with a statement that you might have limited experience in an area and your best thought was one way or another was okay. I struggled to maintain a calm approach and, of course, I indicated my desire to make the army my career, though I really wasn't sure of that yet. I thought I had done okay when it was over, but I really had no idea.

Two weeks later I got the word. I had passed and was being scheduled to move down to Fort Benning, Georgia, to enter OCS during the first week of June 1965. I was excited as could be, and I was scared to death. I had been told the wash-out rate could be as high as 50 percent. I was told that if there was a doubt about my drive and ability, I would be out. A lot of this came from my NCO friends on the ranges, who all knew NCOs who had tried the course and washed out. They weren't trying to scare me. Rather, I felt that they were encouraging me to focus and get it together. I was going to do just that.

CHAPTER 6
FORT BENNING: OCS

Fort Benning is the infantry headquarters of the U.S. Army. I felt immediately upon my arrival that I was in a place deeply important to the real combat work of the army. In addition to infantry OCS, it is the home for the parachute training school; the ranger school; the infantry officers' career course; the infantry tactics school; and, at that time, of the army's entry into modern helicopter warfare. The 1st Cavalry Division (Airmobile) was in the process of organizing to go to Vietnam.

My assignment was to the 55th Company of the OCS Battalion, and my class was labeled 10-65, which meant that when we finished we would be the tenth class to graduate in 1965. The six OCS companies, 50 through 55, were housed in modern three-story brick buildings with the candidates assigned two to a room.

As we assembled in front of the 55th Company entrance on a Sunday afternoon it was a very mixed picture of candidates. I estimated that more than half were around twenty-two years old and as new to the army as I was. We were mainly PFCs and Spec 4s, many with college degrees and some who had not completed their college work. The other group was composed of career NCOs, many of them E-6 staff sergeants nearer to thirty years of age whose performance was such that their commanding officers in active line units had encouraged them to apply to OCS. The group assembled that afternoon comprised more than two hundred and twenty-five soldiers.

As I looked around, I saw that some of the NCO candidates were clearly not in shape, and I remembered that I had been told that over half would wash out. The 55th Company commander, a captain, gave us a welcome speech and reaffirmed that as many as half of the group wouldn't be there in six months. As he talked, ten young lieutenants, all wearing spit-shined boots, polished helmets, immaculate fatigue uniforms, and very grim expressions, stalked the files of officer candidates to look us over. These men were our tactical officers, whom we called "tacs". They were the men who would rule our world for the next six months. This first afternoon, as they patrolled the ranks, they asked a question here or there, but for the moment they adopted a very low-key manner, which made them even more scary to me.

We were issued new uniforms without rank designation and told that past rank was gone and we were all now officer candidates. We were organized into platoons, each with acting platoon leader and squad leader assignments made; assigned roommates; directed on how to organize our rooms; had dinner; and were told to hit the sack, with "lights out" at 10:00 p.m. Wake-up call would be at 6 a.m. All of the above was done in a low-key manner, but the general feeling amongst all the officer candidates was that something was wrong. This was much too civilized. This couldn't last. We were right.

All hell broke loose 4:30 a.m. The tac officers rampaged into the rooms, screaming at us to get our lazy asses out of bed, get cleaned up, get the room in order, get into the uniform of the day, and fall into ranks in front of the company building. Only we weren't allowed to do any of the above as we were stopped in the hallway, told to brace against the wall and assume the position of attention. "Suck in that fat chin, you worm." The harassment was trumpeted at the of the top of the tacs' lung power, accompanied by a good spit into your face in accomplishing the need to get maximum volume. It was meant to be insane, and it was.

When the company finally had fallen into ranks beneath the lights in front of the building, officer candidates were pulled from the ranks, right and left, and told to "drop and give me twenty" push-ups. Then we were told we were in the wrong uniforms and to get back inside, get into the right uniform, and be back in ranks in five minutes. Impossible, of course, especially with all two hundred and twenty-five of us fighting and elbowing the others out of our way as we ran to comply. Even then, we were confronted once again by the tac officers, who braced us against the walls while screaming about some imagined infraction. It was total, fear-inducing, mind-boggling chaos, as it was meant to be. We changed uniforms again, dropped for push-ups multiple times, went for a long "welcome to OCS" run, and assembled back at the company building, all in the dark. We were finally at attention in ranks when reveille was sounded at 6:00 a.m. This introduction was modeled on the West Point hell week, and it was indeed hell. We had only six months more to go.

We marched in to breakfast under continuing harassment, and no one managed to eat in any satisfactory manner. I noticed some officer candidates receiving quiet counseling on the sidelines. We would learn that when a tac was yelling at you that was the way things should be. The quiet talk was a bad sign. Some soldiers had expressed doubts and were already throwing in the towel.

The harassment continued unabated. It was clear that the system was designed to encourage us to quit, the sooner the better. One important element for me was that the physical side of things was no problem. I couldn't understand why any soldier would dream they could come to OCS in anything less than the best of shape. We continued to be pressured in every area as we started classes in chemical warfare, tactical nuclear warfare, the military code of justice, and numerous other topics. We were introduced to the twenty-four-hour day.

Tac officer: "Candidate X, why didn't you complete the chemical warfare write-up you were directed to have ready today?"

Officer candidate X: "Sir, I just didn't have enough time in yesterday's schedule, sir."

Tac officer: "Candidate X, how much sleep did you get last night?"

Officer candidate X: "Sir, seven hours, sir."

Tac officer, leaning back with a maliciously appraising look for the ignorant one: "So, you're telling me you wasted seven hours having fantasy dreams when you could have been fulfilling your assignment?"

Officer candidate X, realizing he'd walked into it and quickly reassessing his position, hoping he could grovel and work his way out of this: "Sir, yes, sir. I failed to properly utilize my time, sir. It won't happen again, sir."

Tac officer, if he's feeling warm and cozy: "You're a worm, Candidate X. I don't know why the army is bothering with you. Drop and give me twenty, and then get out of my sight."

We soon learned that, in a respectable time after lights out, thirty minutes or so, we could take our work down to the latrine, where the lights were on all night, and do our studies for an additional hour or two or three. I found the studies were not a problem for me, and I ended up helping some of the other candidates, usually the former NCOs, with their assignments. It wasn't that they were of lesser intelligence. Rather, it soon hit me that they had forgotten how to study, while for those of us who had recently been in college study was second nature.

Twelve weeks was the major demarcation line in the six-month course. We had dropped quite a number of officer candidates by then, possibly as many as sixty. There was a twelve-week panel, which reviewed officer candidates from our class who were considered to be on the margin in performance. This was a group of around twenty candidates. Some were dropped and some were allowed to recycle to a new OCS class that would be starting soon. This meant that if they made it all the way through the second class, as a friend of mine did, they would have spent nine months in OCS before graduating, including the toughest three months twice. Now, that's real determination.

We were evaluated on physical ability, class scores, and leadership. The leadership evaluations were rendered by the tac officers, but they included peer evaluations we were made to do on each other as we rotated in the temporary platoon and squad leadership positions. The physical scores and class scores were posted, and we paid close attention to them. This was a competition. I had learned that peer competition is always the way it is in the military. The bottom guys are dropped. I soon found that I had no trouble being rated in the top 5 percent of physical testing and in the top five guys in the class test scores.

The company designated a group of soldiers to be called the Brains and Brawn Platoon, in which I was included. They set up a special "no harassment table" for us in the dining hall. Seated there were twelve guys who were at the top in both physical training and class scores. I liked having that distinction. I wouldn't know until we graduated what my leadership ranking would be, but I was comfortable it would be near the top. In fact, I hoped for a top 10-percent position but I couldn't be sure. The college guys in our class dominated the class scores and did well for the most part in the physical tests. The former NCOs made better impressions in the leadership positions because they were used to ordering others around in the military manner and were louder and more decisive in doing so.

The tac officers eased off somewhat during the final three months of OCS. After four months had passed, we started to get occasional overnight passes to go into Columbia, Georgia. I didn't go, but one of my buddies, a good-looking college graduate from Kansas, went into town and managed to get a date with a local girl. He came back very discouraged. "No chance" he said, "They're all hardcore Baptists."

As time passed the training began to get really interesting. We learned how to direct a rifle platoon in the attack and a rifle platoon in defense. We studied and practiced the tactics of ambushes, the use of the rifle company's 81mm mortars, and adjusted artillery fire, among other field exercises. As the months went by we focused increasingly on Vietnam. In October and November, the news of the fighting in the Ia Drang Valley and the terrible casualties taken by the 1st Cavalry Division reached us and shocked everyone in The Infantry School. One of the field exercises had us occupying and searching a mock Vietnamese farm village in which NCO advisors who had served in Vietnam taught us what to look for in terms of booby traps and places to hide weapons. We did an intensive session of map-and-compass work, including an escape-and-evasion exercise. I found this interesting as I had developed a good feel for using maps and a compass, and this really boosted my overall confidence. We got to fire new weapons, including the new M-16 for the first time. It was a light assault rifle with a high rate of fire. I loved it even though we were warned repeatedly that it needed to be kept clean to prevent jamming. I got to fire the 50.-caliber heavy machine gun and found the long reach of the weapon very impressive.

We were finally on the verge of graduation. I had let up on my studies a bit but was still in the top ten candidates, and I knew I had that position locked. My concern now was to top out on the physical side. The army physical training test had a maximum score for five events of five hundred points. I had been flirting with the top all along and scored four hundred eighty points several times. This was a score that the OCS hierarchy really paid attention to. All the tac officers wanted their platoons to earn the top score, and the company commander wanted his company to earn the top score, all for bragging rights within the OCS world.

One of the events was a mock grenade throw. It wasn't how far you threw the grenade as much as distance *and* accuracy. There was a small circle about twenty-five meters out. Put it in that circle and you got a hundred points. I had been just outside the circle several times and now took the time to practice. I was determined to get that hundred points and max the test.

The day of the final test, about a week before graduation, was a big deal. The company commander came out and promised weekend passes for the fiver-hundred- point guys, and we were all encouraged to "put out" for the best possible team score. I was nervous but feeling good. I had gotten my mile run times down under six minutes, which in combat boots is okay. The event that would make it for me was the grenade toss. Somehow, it all came together. I maxed the events I normally did, and I put the grenade in the hundred-point circle. In the mile run I came in at 5:50 minutes, which did the job. The only event left was the high bars, which consisted of twelve overhead bars you had to swing along monkey-style up and back three times for a max of seventy-two bars to get a hundred points. I had good upper body strength and had done this several times. I was feeling good. I had my max score in the bag.

When I went over to the bars for my turn to test, the tac officer in charge was talking to an officer candidate from his platoon. This candidate was a college kid who had run way under six minutes in the mile, and there was talk of his breaking five minutes, a possible OCS record. This tac officer badly wanted the record. I got his attention and asked, "May I start now, sir?" The tac officer looked over and waved me to start, so off I went.

The key to the bars is to get and keep your rhythm while swinging. I soon had the flow of it and had no trouble doing the three trips. As I was making the final return trip I felt so good, I thought "Why not go for another round?" but then I thought, "No, you got it. Just finish."

I finished, dropped off the bars, and shouted to the tac officer, "Sir, done, sir." He looked over at me as if annoyed that I had interrupted his conversation with his pet student and said, "Not good enough, Crowley, you're one round short." I was astounded. I came close to exploding. "You asshole," I thought, "I'm busting my ass and you're neglecting your duty." My face must have gotten real red because the tac office now gave me his full attention, watching me closely to see what I would say. I told him, "Sir, you're mistaken. I did the full seventy-two rungs." He turned to look at me full-on, tilted his head as he looked at me, possibly wondering what this officer candidate was going to do. He said, "If you want to go on again, you can have another chance."

At the end of the day of testing and having just finished one round, it was very doubtful I could do the full cycle again. It was a test of my self-control, but I wasn't about to mar my conduct record at that point in the cycle by letting this guy know he was an asshole. I swallowed my disappointment and said, "No, sir. Thank you, sir," and got the hell out of there. It was another four-eighty score.

All the scores were posted just before graduation. I had some consolation by being included in the final Brains and Brawn Platoon. I thought that was a pretty good group to be in. My buddy who struck out with the Baptist girl was one of two guys to max the physical training test. The leadership scores were another story.

My leadership ranking only put me in the 70th percentile, or the top 30 percent of the class to look at it more positively. I was shocked. This really took the wind out of my sails. OCS did a good job. By this time, the whole class was a very self-confident group of young officers. I was certainly more then sure of myself, perhaps floating on the edge of arrogance.

This evaluation set me to thinking: What had I done wrong or not done that resulted in this, what I considered to be a lesser evaluation? It took me some time to think it through. The bottom line is that, while it's nice to excel in class and the physical challenges, the really important value in a military officer is leadership ability. This lower grading set off a long period of self-examination on my part, which would continue right up to the time I arrived in Vietnam.

There were two critical factors in the evaluation. One very important thing in the military is height. I'm not short at 5 feet, 10 inches, but I noticed that the parades were led, in many senses, in the military by the tallest guys. The guys over six feet tall had an advantage in what the military and West Point today call, "military presence." I think it means when the very tall guy walks into the room, or gives a briefing, you pay more attention. It should be noted that military presence has nothing to do with military leadership ability, but the United States military to this day continues to conflate the two. I would learn that combat clarifies the issue. In combat, it's what you do. Height is not a determinant of performance. My buddy who was recycled to my class after twelve weeks with another OCS class was 5 feet, 6 inches, tall, which I believe caused his low leadership rating. In Vietnam, he led from the front and his platoon worshipped him.

Secondly, and again this is a hallmark of the military at all times, there is the *hooah* factor. I'm not a hooah guy. In general, I noted that it was more the former NCOs, used to army ways, who put out a lot of WETSU (we eat this shit up) during hard times and loud rah-rah talk, who scored leadership points through this form of projection. Again, in combat, I found no correlation to leadership ability with noisemaking.

For all that, I couldn't dismiss my ranking by just saying my evaluation was wrong based on these factors. I thought I had to look at how I approached communicating goals and needs to the troops when I was in charge. It became clear to me that I was too low key and needed to increase the intensity of my communication and explore that thing called "military presence."

* * *

With graduation and receipt of my gold bars there was one other quick stop to be made, and that was parachute school, which started immediately after we graduated. Virtually the entire class attended. It was a fun three weeks, though I will admit the night before our first jump my roommate (he of the Baptist lady disappointment) and I stayed up late to reassure one another that we weren't scared.

One incident that has stuck with me to this day occurred on graduation day, when we got our jump wings. I had been a stick leader, meaning I led a string of about fifteen officers and enlisted men and was responsible for organizing them before we loaded on the planes. I also led the jump out the door.

The morning we got our jump wings one of the young enlisted men, a young slick-sleeve Black soldier from the Bronx, who was just out of advanced infantry school, came up to me just beaming with pride. He told me, "Lieutenant Crowley, sir, I'm just so proud. I'm the first member of my family to go through jump school."

I couldn't help but smile back. I told him, "You've done it, soldier. Your family will be proud of you." Then it struck me that he looked awfully young. He was only about 5 feet, 7 inches, tall and was painfully skinny. I asked him then how old he was. He was still smiling and pumped up over completing parachute school. His answer was that he was seventeen. All I could think of was that I was sure that, after airborne training, this kid was on his way to Vietnam, if not immediately then within six months for sure. My mind flashed on the terrible casualties the 1st Cavalry had recently taken. The war machine needed fresh bodies, especially infantrymen, and I got the terrible feeling that this young man would be dead before the end of the year. I kept my smile on my face, wished him good luck and said maybe we'll serve together again down the road. But I had a sick feeling in my stomach and have ever since whenever I remember him. I hope he made it. But I doubt it.

CHAPTER 7
FORT GORDON: JUNGLE EXPERT SCHOOL

We were all going to Vietnam. That had been made clear every week during our OCS training. The issue for the army was getting us into their cycle of replacements, especially with units organizing in the States. Some infantry divisions that had not been active since the Korean War were being brought back to active status and needed NCOs and officers to fill out the leadership positions. About half of my class went to these divisions while the rest of us were sent to training camps to work as training officers until it was time for us to go to Vietnam. To my disappointment, I ended up getting orders to Fort Gordon, Georgia, where I would be assigned as a training officer overseeing some of the ranges used to teach E-1s the initial steps to soldiering. This would include many of the same lessons I had learned a year and a half earlier and then had assisted in at Fort Jackson a year earlier.

I decided one good thing this would give me was an opportunity to look at how well I conducted myself in front of the soldiers. Specifically, I jumped at the chance to take on the lead instructor's role myself. This involved getting up in front of the classes and delivering the lesson of the day, whatever that might be. I took the lesson plans and practiced at home before the mirror. My being out front was not a small matter because the instruction on the ranges was closely monitored by senior officers involved in preparing and overseeing the instruction and by visiting inspection officers. The NCOs, as always in the army, were the ones who really ran things. Officers were there to sign off on paperwork, take the blame if something went wrong, and fulfill roles designated for them by the NCOs. Officers, especially junior officers, came and went, but the NCOs stayed. Several of the junior officers I spoke with who filled similar positions liked the fact that they were basically along for the ride with little direct responsibility. I didn't like it, but I accepted it as long as I got what I called stage time, a chance to speak as an instructor in front of the troops, where I worked to improve my projection and speaking ability. I practiced, worked, and got good enough that the senior NCOs accepted my taking part in their productions.

For all my good intentions, my reflection on leadership eventually led to a clash with the system that was in place, the only time in my service that I was reprimanded by a senior officer. At one of the ranges I worked on we had a newly commissioned ROTC-sourced infantry lieutenant. He wore somewhat thick glasses, was about my height, and painfully skinny. He projected no confidence at all. At that time in the military, there was no special platoon leaders course for college grads or West Pointers when they were commissioned. They just went into specialized training, such as parachute school, and then to duty assignments. One of the advantages of OCS was that it was at the heart of all specialized training for platoon and company leadership. It was at that time still a six-month course and had not yet been shortened to a three-month course for the Vietnam War, though that would happen soon. All of us who came out of OCS at that time were confident to the point of cocky. This guy was the opposite, and I was shocked. The thought that he might find himself leading a rifle platoon in Vietnam in a matter of months dismayed me. My immediate feeling was that we had to find ways to build his confidence.

The NCO in charge of the range didn't want the lieutenant doing anything in front of the troops. I argued that he should be given an instructor's role and that I would work with him to bring his presentation up to the necessary standard. The NCO again disagreed, but I overruled him, worked with the new lieutenant, and found a time to put him on stage. He was scared, but he did a presentable job and was grateful to me when it was over. The NCO in charge wasn't grateful.

The next thing I knew I was called in front of a major, the executive officer of the training battalion. He asked why I had overruled the NCO in charge. I explained my reasoning, that I thought we had an obligation to the young officer that overrode considerations of the visibility of our stage excellence before the basic training soldiers. The major disagreed, sided with the NCO, and said it would have been embarrassing if a senior officer had inspected during the ROTC officer's presentation. I was put on restricted duty for three days, overseeing the painting of some buildings by a group of enlisted men who had gotten into trouble themselves. I was really upset, but, at the same time, a bit grateful. I had learned something. This is what the peacetime army was all about, putting on a show and passing inspections. I was not interested.

I wanted out of Fort Gordon and my make-work job, so I volunteered for army aviation. I was sent for a test ride in an observation chopper. The pilot, who had had the Plexiglas doors taken off of the H-13 bubble chopper, proceeded to take me up and do a series of banks so that I was looking straight down at the ground a thousand feet below. It was great fun. He went ahead and landed after a few minutes and I asked, "Is that it?" He nodded and laughed. I guess the idea was to see if I showed signs of fear of altitude or got sick. I hadn't, so I passed.

While I was waiting to hear about flight school, we had a visit from a major who was with the Infantry Branch personnel office at the Pentagon. His nominal reason for visiting was to educate the junior infantry officers on base about the process of keeping their records and efficiency reports at the Pentagon, but it soon became apparent that his real goal was to get the officers to volunteer to end their current assignments at Fort Gordon for immediate assignment to Vietnam. Obviously, the Vietnam troop deployment ramp-up was being accelerated. I wanted out of Fort Gordon, an army backwater that was draining me of energy. My classmates and I had come out of OCS ready to lead a bayonet charge, so I was not happy to be working with the end-of-career officers stuck on a shelf at Fort Gordon and whose biggest worry was the next inspection. I spoke privately with the major and told him that I had one desire, if possible. I wanted to go to the 101st Airborne Division in Vietnam. He said, "No problem, Lieutenant. Sign here." So I signed.

A few weeks later, I got orders to fixed-wing flight school at Fort Rucker, Alabama. Other officers were pounding me on the back, congratulating me. I learned that this was somehow preferred to rotary wing helicopter flight school as it meant I would start by flying single-engine observation planes and could move up to flying the Mohawk, the army's new twin-engine observation plane. The celebration lasted about three days, and then I received a set of orders assigning me to Vietnam via a stopover at the jungle expert school in Panama. I asked the personnel officer what that meant, and he told me it was very simple: Vietnam took precedence. Forget flight school until after Vietnam.

In late August, I was given orders for a week's leave at home in Milwaukee prior to going on down to Panama and then back to Dover Air Force Base, Delaware, where I would catch a plane to Vietnam.

I had a good but confusing home leave in that I soon hooked up with the guys I had left behind, those who had gone to college and those who had entered the trades. They had no clue about my world and no interest or understanding of the military and Vietnam. Actually, they represented most of America at that time and, as I would learn later, that was a terrible portent of political problems to come. With the Draft running at full steam, a lot of young guys were going into the service. One of my younger brothers had been drafted and was serving as a military policeman in Germany. Another younger brother would enlist in the marines. My older brother had already served four years in the air force.

We had several divisions on the ground in Vietnam by then, and the nightly news routinely displayed scenes of fire fights and wounded soldiers and civilians.

My older sister and her husband drove me to O'Hare airport in Chicago, and we had a cup of coffee before my flight carried me south to Panama. It was a grim setting and a very quiet cup of coffee. Of course, I told them not to worry, I knew what I was doing, I'd had the best of training.

The jungle school was normally a three-week course, now shortened to two weeks due to the need to get troops quickly on to Vietnam. We had more than two hundred junior officers and NCOs in the class, divided into five-man teams. I was a team leader overseeing four NCOs.

Panama is near the Equator and the jungle there is the real thing. It was hot, humid double-canopy forest in many places, and the geography includes rivers and swamps, as well as what we called mountains, which I guess were only about 1,500 feet or so high but which seemed higher when you started at sea level. I was comfortable doing field exercises and camping in the forests in America. The darkness and difficulty of the jungle setting was a greater challenge. I was never comfortable. We built rain shelters, ate snakes, and undertook one amphibious landing, which had us loading on landing craft during the early morning dark and hitting the beach at sunrise. We were constantly on the move.

Two exercises got my special attention. The first was a night compass course. I was really intrigued. How the hell are we going to use a compass and navigate through the jungle when we couldn't see?

We were able to use a red filtered flashlight, and the markers on the course were set just fifty to sixty meters apart. Nevertheless, the night and the jungle were absolutely black. I really had my doubts, but, amazingly enough, I found that if I remained disciplined in my approach and relied absolutely on my compass and my pacing that I was able to find the markers and complete the course successfully. This boosted my confidence in my map and compass work once again and was enormously helpful in preparing me for what was to come in the months ahead.

The second exercise that made an impression on me was the escape-and-evasion course, which was a two-day exercise. We were given a briefing on the terrain and the goal, which was to reach a safe base at the mouth of a river. To get to the safe base, which it was said friendly forces held, we would be released in what was termed enemy country, in a swamp on the far side of the mountain range. I took the map and compass lead for my team as we were released in late morning, and we led off into the swamp. It was uncomfortable and tough going as we were at times waist-deep in the swamp, but that was the direction the compass was taking us, and the compass ruled. It wasn't until the sun was setting that we got into shallower water and finally, just after dark, started to walk on firm ground. In due course, we climbed through the jungle growth and up the steep hillside.

It started to rain heavily, so we agreed, for safety's sake to, stop and spend the night in a small opening in the jungle on the side of the hill. There we sat in a circle, nearly touching each other, under the cover of our ponchos, as the rain poured down on us in the black of the night. A fire wasn't possible due to the escape-and-evasion guidelines, but it was so wet I doubt we could have started and maintained a fire in any case.

We were a miserable group. We tried to sleep, but around midnight we heard a terrible scream from the jungle just yards away. It shook us all awake and scared the hell out of us. Then a moment or two later, the scream was repeated from a different direction. These screams went on for a while before we worked it out. A jungle cat, possibly a black panther, which was present in this jungle, was stalking us. The cat was probably trying to figure out what the unfamiliar scent meant. There was nothing we could do. We just waited. After thirty minutes or so, the cat decided we weren't food and went away.

In the morning, we headed up to the top of the hill, made contact with the "friendly" natives who were in our script and were guided to the river we had to cross. We made a raft, achieved our crossing of the river, and successfully completed the escape-and-evasion course.

We were graded as a team for some sections of the course—building our jungle huts, for example—and individually for other sections, an important one being the map and compass work.

The day we graduated, I was told that the individual scores were posted in the school office. I was hopeful that I had topped the grade charts and went over to take a look. I got to the office just in time to see the officer in charge of the school presenting a ceremonial sword to the top scorer in the course, another infantry lieutenant. I looked at the score sheet and saw that I had come in second once again. He had 993 points out of a possible one thousand, and I had 992. So be it. It was time to get on the road to Vietnam.

The next morning, as we were clearing out of the school, as I was going up the stairs to get my duffel bag, I passed Al Guyer, an OCS classmate, going down the same stairs. At the bottom of the stairs, he turned and yelled back at me, "Hey, Crowley, is there anything difficult to this course." I told him, "No, nothing compared to what we've already been through." That was it. That was the last time I saw Al.

I got my bag and headed for the door. I had some long plane rides to get through, and Vietnam was my next stop.

CHAPTER 8
CROSSING THE RUBICON

It's a toss-up as to what hits you first as you deplane. That's what the military calls it, deplane. You don't leave or exit the aircraft, you "deplane". Mixed impressions assault you, one after the other, each fighting for supremacy in your dazed consciousness as it tries to recuperate from more than thirty hours of air travel. It's the heat that wins the battle. It's definitely the tropical heat, humidity, the instant full-body sweat that takes the starch out of your uniform in seconds. A close second impression is the strong smell of aviation gas, JP 4, whose acrid odor is amplified by the heat. A third is the noise. Choppers are lifting; planes are landing; fighter jets are taking off, their afterburners kicking in. Large civilian passenger and cargo airplanes, fighter and ground-support jets are all taking their turns. Then you notice the very prominent gun emplacements and the variety of uniformed armed men walking around, all carrying their personal weapons. Buildings are sheltered behind sandbag walls to catch the shrapnel from a mortar or rocket attack. Machine gun emplacements speckle the edges of the tarmac. It's a hot, smelly, noisy, busy place, as foreign as it can be and reeking of imminent danger. Welcome to Tan Son Nhut Air Base, Saigon, Vietnam. Wartime.

It was September 1966, and I was a junior infantry officer, a rifle platoon leader just months out of parachute school at Fort Benning and days out of the Jungle Expert School in Panama. The written orders I had been given didn't assign me to any specific unit in Vietnam. I was instead ordered to report to an administrative office at Tan Son Nhut, which allocated soldiers to various military units according to the need for replacements with differing skills. Your assignment depended on what the military calls your Military Occupational Specialty, MOS. My MOS was 71542, an airborne-qualified infantry small-unit leader, which means a rifle platoon leader taking forty infantry soldiers into combat. The MOS for the enlisted infantrymen was 11 Bravo. Not that I couldn't be assigned to any of a number of other positions, depending on the "needs of the service," as they say.

An air force noncommissioned officer directed our group to grab our duffel bags, then led us to an area nearby called Camp Alpha, which was the all-services replacement center. We would spend the night here.

In the morning, we would turn in our orders and wait for our fates to be decided. Each of us wondered which unit he would go to and what job assignment he would be given.

The NCO pointed us toward a wooden barracks with a tin roof that would be our hooch, as we called it, for the night. He told us to leave our bags on the bunks inside and then pointed the way to an aluminum Quonset hut, where next morning we would drop off the orders that had brought us to Vietnam. We were given nothing to do until then, so we simply marked time.

It was a long, uncomfortable, thoughtful night for all of us. The excited chatter that had filled the civilian charter flight that brought us over simply faded away. I remember some dumb lieutenant on the plane saying he was going to make sure he was awarded a Bronze Star, at least. He felt that this award was the minimum requirement to assure his career prospects. Now that foolish talk was a thing of the past. The reality was here and now, and no one had much to say.

The next morning, after breakfast, we all walked slowly over to the Quonset hut housing the assignments unit, the papers which had brought us to Vietnam in hand, to be exchanged for our in-county orders. There was no talk at all. Apprehension filled the air. Even those whose MOS would put them in a support role were nervous; they didn't want to go to one of the infantry division base camps located in jungle or coastal areas well away from Saigon, where the chance of rocket or mortar attacks was high.

There are times in life when you are confronted with a decision that will affect the remaining course of your existence. Sometimes, maybe many times, the need for such a choice arises abruptly. For me, such a moment came on that first morning of my tour. Assignment to Vietnam was inevitable for an infantry officer, so I had volunteered for duty there, hoping to be allocated to the 101st Airborne, which was considered one of the U.S. Army's elite divisions. That assignment was what I had been promised by the recruiting officer from the Pentagon who had visited my base in the States. In any case, it was a given that I was to go to one of the infantry divisions and receive an assignment as a rifle platoon leader.

There was a shortage of junior officers to take up the front-line positions in Vietnam. The main reason for this was that officers (and medics, I should note) were the prime targets when Viet Cong or North Vietnamese units engaged American. units. At the time, the conventional wisdom said that six out of ten rifle platoon leaders would be killed or wounded during a one-year tour in Vietnam. I don't know how real that figure was, but it was the one that was commonly bandied about. In any event, there was a constant need for new rifle platoon leaders.

Another reason was that many in the upper military echelons considered Vietnam a handy training ground for future high-ranking leaders. It was army policy to rotate officers out of positions with a direct combat role after six months of duty. This was to give as many officers as possible efficiency reports in "combat" duty roles in order to enhance their career prospects.

Enlisted men didn't rate such treatment; they had to stick it out on the line for the full duration of their one-year tour unless they had been wounded three times, which was the other ticket out. It is often said that life is not fair, and the military does its best to apply that truism. There was a popular joke after the war. Whenever someone asked "How could you Americans lose in Vietnam when you were there for fifteen years?" the answer was, "We weren't there for fifteen years; we were there for one year fifteen times." Or, in terms of combat leadership positions, six months thirty times. The VC or NVA forces were there for the duration, however many generations it might take. I was to find that it made an enormous difference to their combat effectiveness.

Early that morning, as I made my way over to the administration office in Camp Alpha to discover my fate, I was filled with a good deal of apprehension as well as curiosity. Which infantry division I was to go to, and thus which part of the country I would serve my tour in, were the main questions on my mind. I was preoccupied with finding out. Thus, it was with a bit of shock that I heard my name being called out as I neared the building, "Lieutenant Crowley, Lieutenant Crowley! Over here, sir!" I looked, and just inside the office, sitting at a side table, was a staff sergeant (four stripes on his sleeves, three up, one down) whom I knew from my previous service as a training officer at Fort Jackson, South Carolina. I hadn't realized that he had been posted to Vietnam prior to me and I was as surprised to see him as he was to see me.

He rose from his desk and waved me outside the building, where we could talk privately. We asked each other what we were doing there. I told him I was on my way to discover my orders for assignment. He told me that he had been in-country for a month and was assigned to Camp Alpha to carry out administrative duties. He mentioned the name of another, more senior, NCO who had been at Camp Alpha when he arrived and who had pulled strings to get him this very safe assignment, saving him from going out to one of the infantry divisions for possible field duty.

The background on these two NCOs is relevant. They were both men who had been in the army more than fifteen years, so they were in their mid-thirties. They had both served tours as infantrymen in the Korean War. I mentioned previously that I worked with them training new recruits at Fort Jackson. I had gotten along with them well, but they had made it clear they were dedicated to coasting along in their work assignments (today this is called ROAD, retired on active duty). Their goal seemed to be to stay out of trouble, not to attract the attention of officers, and to do the least amount of work possible while putting in the necessary time—twenty years—to claim retirement pay. Now, unwillingly to be sure, they had been drawn into the military maelstrom that was Vietnam and were thus determined to avoid being assigned to field duty.

The NCO who had called me over was very urgent in his manner. "Lieutenant, you don't want to get into that line," he said, pointing to the assignments queue just a few feet away. "You give them your orders and they'll just ship you up to a line unit where you'll get your ass shot off. Give me your papers and I'll do some work in back and get you assigned here to Camp Alpha. It's good duty, Lieutenant, and we get into Saigon as often as we want."

Years later, I would look back on those few seconds and wonder why it was so clear to me that I couldn't take him up on his offer. Possibly it was the ignorance and arrogance of the very young. Also, even though we junior officers on the flight over had been talking about infantry officers having the odds against them, I'm sure we were all under the illusion that it was *other* infantry officers who would have the bad luck and catch the bullet. I should also add that I felt very strongly that I had received the best of training. The military is obsessive about rating every activity in which soldiers are involved, and I was proud to have been in the top 10 percent in every rated category, near the top of every class or course that I had gone through. My mindset was that I was prepared and that I was here in Vietnam to fulfill my duty. In contrast, I stared at the prospect of days spent watching my colleagues, fellow infantry officers, come through the camp to be assigned to combat units while I stood safely by. And I envisioned nights taking the bus into Saigon to get drunk and savor the fruits of my dereliction of duty.

This sounds like a lot to embrace mentally, but it all just flashed through my mind in seconds. I was absolutely clear when I replied, "Thanks, Sarge, but I'll go through the line." He looked shocked and repeated, "Don't do it, sir. You'll be sorry. People are getting killed out there." I just told him, "I have to go through the line, Sarge. Thanks anyway." He just said okay and went back to his desk.

While I stood in the line waiting to have my orders processed, I watched the soldiers coming out the door. Most were expressionless; they hadn't expected anything special and they hadn't received it. It was guaranteed that any infantry soldier was going up to serve with one of the infantry divisions.

Then an infantry captain came out the door. He was a Special Forces officer and was wearing their signature green beret. He had an angry look on his face and, with a gesture of disgust, he removed the beret and threw it in a trash bin just outside the assignments hut door. The message was clear: the war was changing, there was now less need for Special Forces groups working with the indigenous population, and more need for the "special" troops called "grunts". These were the troops of the regular infantry divisions, and the captain had evidently been allocated to one of those units. It was obvious he felt it was a step down after all his training. After getting over my shock at his reaction, I felt a strange sense of satisfaction and thought, "Come on, Captain, join the rest of us on the line." Now, to be sure, the thought was unfair in that the Special Forces A teams definitely lived life on the edge, serving far out from the security of the main American or ARVN military units that could support them when they came under attack from the NVA or VC. These were, without a doubt, brave men. All the same, his action reaffirmed for me that the primary war effort now belonged with grunts like those in whatever unit I would join.

I continued to wait in line. A few minutes later, I handed my papers to a captain who was processing the officers. He took my orders, looked down at a list he had, and said, "Congratulations, Lieutenant, you'll be going up to the 25th Infantry Division at Cu Chi. There'll be a chopper out on the tarmac this afternoon. Get yourself ready. Come back after lunch to pick up your new orders." He handed my papers over to an enlisted man sitting at the desk nearby and told him to get my orders ready. As for the promised assignment to the 101st Airborne Division, I was slightly disappointed but understood I'd been more than a little foolish to put any faith in a recruitment officer from the Pentagon. This was the reality of the army.

I had crossed the Rubicon. I had no second thoughts, just a willingness to get on with what was to be.

Only as we travel through life and look back can we evaluate properly the impact of the decisions we make along the way. I would certainly pay a price in pain for that decision, and there is no way to know what the cost would have been if I had taken up the well-meaning NCO on his offer. I've always believed it would have been a substantially greater price in the destruction of my self-esteem, with whatever consequences that might have entailed. But we can never know.

It occurred to me much later that I wasn't alone in that process of deciding to follow what I thought was my duty and go toward the sound of the guns. Many, many American warriors did likewise and must in every war. The tale of the 1st Cavalry Division in the battles for the Ia Drang Valley tells us of soldiers who had been sent back to base camp to prepare to leave Vietnam as their overseas service was coming to a close who nonetheless put on their combat gear and caught a chopper back into the fighting when they heard their buddies were in trouble. Some of those men died in that effort to help their buddies. Military units are held together by the devotion with which the soldiers hold to one another.

I caught the chopper that afternoon and was processed through the 25th Infantry Division admin office late in the day. Next, I caught a truck to the headquarters of the 4th Battalion, 9th Infantry Regiment, in the Cu Chi base camp. It was well after dark and too late to check in formally, so I just followed the directions of the duty officer to an empty tent to catch some sleep.

I have learned that much of life is luck. The next morning, when I met the soldiers with whom I would serve, I discovered that I was lucky to have joined one of the U.S. Army's leading infantry divisions. The 25th, or Tropic Lightning, as it is nicknamed from its time in the Pacific in World War II, was normally based in Hawaii. The division had been specially trained for jungle warfare and had been in Vietnam for over six months when I joined as a replacement. That meant that, as a green junior officer, I was in the company of seasoned NCOs and officers who knew the ways of the enemy and the jungle. My decision to stay in the assignments line at Camp Alpha was my responsibility. The luck to land with the 25th was fate. Fittingly, when I was assigned as leader of the 2nd Platoon of Alpha Company, I found that my platoon sergeant, Sergeant First Class Francis Amado, was a native Hawaiian, and further that native Hawaiians sprinkled throughout the 25th were among the best of soldiers we had.

The battalion I was with was unusual in several ways. First, it was part of the 9th Infantry Regiment. (In 1966, a regiment could vary in size from three or four battalions with three or four companies of one hundred and fifty to two hundred soldiers in each.) The regiment's battle history went back to the War of 1812 and encompassed the Mexican War, the wars against the Indian tribes on the Western frontier after the Civil War (including participation in the ill-fated Custer expedition to the Little Big Horn), the relief of Western forces in Peking during the Boxer Rebellion, the Philippine Insurrection at the turn of the century, World War I in France, World War II in Europe, the Korean War (with action at Bloody Ridge and Pork Chop Hill), and now Vietnam. For its efforts during the Boxer Rebellion to relieve the foreign legations in Peking, it was officially nicknamed the Manchu Regiment.

My current battalion, the 4th Battalion, 9th Infantry, had been stationed in Alaska, training as the Army's winter troops, prior to being ordered to Hawaii in January 1966 to become part of the 25th Infantry Division and undergo eight weeks of jungle training.

The 25th Division and my new battalion mobilized for war, with advance units arriving in Vietnam by air as early as January in Pleiku and Cu Chi. My battalion traveled to Vietnam via the port of Vung Tau in April 1966. Thus, besides the native Hawaiians in my platoon, I had an Eskimo and soldiers who had enlisted to be ski troops as well as the usual replacements from all over the States. The platoon was definitely a cross-section of America. For the most part, these soldiers had been together for a year or more and knew and trusted each other. Now it would be my job to earn their trust.

I was operating at one disadvantage when I joined Alpha Company and received my assignment as the 2nd Platoon leader, and that was the absence of an active incumbent in place. Normally, I would have had a few hours with the outgoing platoon leader to go over the background of the platoon sergeant and the squad leaders and discuss any possible issues with the troops. I wasn't given that opportunity.

CHAPTER 9
TRAINING WHEELS

When I arrived in Cu Chi, Alpha Company was not in the division base area; it was in a forward base camp just outside a village nearer the Mekong Delta in Long An Province. On the second morning in Cu Chi, I hitched a chopper ride down to the company position and reported to Captain Neilsen, my new commanding officer. He welcomed me, asked a little about my background, and then told me Platoon Sergeant Amado would brief me. Then he went on to say that the current activity was basically night ambush patrols run from the base camp with the platoons taking turns. My platoon wasn't scheduled to go out at present, so I would have a few days at least to talk with Sergeant Amado and the squad leaders and learn the background of the troops in the platoon, who numbered around thirty-five at the time. The captain then called for Sergeant Amado to come over to his tent. He introduced us and told Amado to take me down and introduce me to the guys in the platoon.

The company position struck me as unusual in that it was sited literally on the edge of a farm village, with the farm huts so close they were bumping up against the barbed wire enclosure. Alpha Company's bunkers and ramshackle hooches, made out of artillery ammo boxes, had been built by the troops themselves.

I was to discover find that, in the Mekong Delta region, the soldiers' bunkers and hooches bumping up against the farm villager's huts was a matter of necessity because there was so little dry ground on which to put a company position. The entire landscape was barely above sea level and was underwater almost permanently when it was being used to grow rice.

As I left the captain's tent with Sergeant Amado to meet the platoon, we came across a bizarre sight. No one saw us coming because all the guys were transfixed by one of the farmers as he attempted to breed his pigs in his back yard, right next to the perimeter wire. The farmer was struggling to hold the sow still so the hog could mount her and do the job. Both pigs were squealing to beat the band. Most of the guys were yelling encouragement to the hog to get on and get the job done. Sergeant Amado looked at me and laughed. My introduction to the platoon would have to wait until after the breeding was done.

When I was finally introduced to the platoon as we assembled around the hooches, I kept my talk short and simple. I could see by their eyes that they were apprehensive. It was the reality for the enlisted soldier. A poor platoon leader could get you killed.

I told them that I was glad to be with the 25th Infantry Division. I understood the division had an excellent reputation and Captain Neilsen had said that this was a solid platoon. Actually, he hadn't said that, but I threw it in anyway. I told them that I would work closely with Sergeant Amado and that my goal was for all of us to just do the best job we could and to get everybody home. I told them I had to talk with Sergeant Amado and the squad leaders but that I would talk with every one of them again over the next few weeks. That was it. It wasn't an inspiring talk, but I thought it was important that they hear me say that getting them all home was one of my goals, because there was no doubt that it was *their* principal goal.

I had a couple of days at that camp to get a feel for the company routine. I was included in briefing the patrols that were sent out at night so I would come to understand what the army called the standard operating procedure (SOP).

Then, on the third day, my 2nd Platoon was sent on a day patrol to look over an area in which another company patrol had ambushed some VC traveling at night near the intersection of a dirt road and a canal. Canals crisscrossed the entire Delta region; they were the main highways for transporting goods and, in the case of the VC, men and weapons to different areas. At the ambush site, the road was still littered with M-16 shell casings. Farther on, nearer the canal, some blood-stained bandages had been left behind by the wounded VC. Those items got my attention.

I was now close to the war. In Vietnam, the front lines were everywhere. This site had been the front line a few nights before and could be again. The captain had laid out a patrol route, which, on the way back, skirted another section of the road designated as that night's ambush site. I checked with Sergeant Amado and he concurred that this was the site we were to return to after dark and set up an ambush for any VC traveling the road.

Back at camp, I reported to Captain Neilsen and he went over the map and operations orders. I was to take a fifteen-man patrol out about an hour after dark, move down the road, and then veer off it on some rice paddy dikes to set up an ambush. I briefed the two NCOs who would be going along so they could brief theirs squads in detail. This was all old stuff for them. The only thing new was that I told them I would lead the way. Neither of them liked that. They wanted me back in the middle of the file so one of them and the point man could get us to the site. They were so strong on it that I partially compromised. I would let two guys lead point and then I would follow along.

My heart pounded as we walked out through the wire. After all my training, it was now real. The site was not far, possibly only one kilometer from the base. We set up within an hour of leaving camp, and that was it. We sat on the wet mud of the rice paddy dike and strained to see or hear anything in the total darkness. We had a good ten hours of darkness to go before sun-up and the walk back to camp. We were to call in a situation report (SITREP) every hour via the radio. If we didn't report on schedule, the RTO at the base would prompt my RTO. If we felt our location might be compromised by talking, we were allowed to key the mike twice, called breaking squelch, to show that all was okay.

The mosquitoes ate us alive. It was the longest ten hours of my life until then, but the dark hours eventually passed.

As the sun rose, we roused ourselves and walked back through the wire into camp. Breakfast was soon ready. The custom was that guys coming back from night patrol got to go to the head of the chow line and eat first, clean up, and hit the sack for a few hours before the hot sun made sleep impossible.

What I didn't understand at the time, and wouldn't until a couple of months down the road, as I gained more experience and understanding, was how lucky I was to join Alpha Company while it was posted at this site in the Delta. We were the first U.S. forces into the Delta. The VC were still moving cautiously, not yet sure how to take on the U.S. forces, who were heavily supported by artillery and air. Essentially, the ambush patrol the captain had arranged for me to lead was a patrol on "training wheels." Our ambush site was only a short distance from the camp, in an area short of where the action had occurred a few nights previously. All that made the likelihood of our getting lost or making contact very low. Captain Neilsen was looking out for the troops more then I was, but we both benefited. I imagine the experienced NCOs I was with understood at the time what was going on, but the green lieutenant didn't. Thank you, Captain Neilsen.

The captain called on my platoon again a few days later. It seems that the higher powers in Saigon had decided that it was important for U.S. units to run joint activities and joint operations with ARVN units. I believe the idea was that the presence of the U.S. forces would encourage the ARVN units, which were thought to be timid in their approach to operations against the VC. In the military way, my division and the battalions within it were being tasked to initiate such activities and make them part of the monthly reports to Saigon.

There was a South Vietnamese infantry company in a shady, tree-lined encampment in the same district Alpha Company was in, several kilometers away from our camp. My platoon was ordered to take up positions within the ARVN camp so this could be reported as a joint operation in the battalion's monthly report. Afterwards, I would think that Captain Neilsen was easing me into operations as this was another assignment that I felt had a low probability of contact.

The VC never knowingly went into combat when the status of the enemy had just changed. Their operational method was to study the enemy unit and make sure they knew exactly the numbers and types of weapons they were taking on before they attacked. The exception to this was if a unit made an air assault directly into or adjacent to positions the VC were using as a camp. When my platoon joined the ARVN unit, we presented a significant change in the tactical situation and the VC, if planning an attack, would wait several days to be sure the situation had stabilized and they had all the information they needed before they attacked. With the addition of my platoon, we had more than one hundred soldiers in the camp.

As a green platoon leader, I had no awareness of all this. I was simply concerned with getting along with the ARVN captain in charge of the camp and have him report our night with his unit as a positive event. He was happy to accept us and told me that he wanted my soldiers to share the camp's guard duty during the night. I readily agreed.

It got dark at 7:00 p.m., and two of my guys were assigned to take the 10:00 p.m.-to-midnight shift. After that, two more were to take the midnight-to 2:00 a.m.-shift.

I let one of my squad leaders set the guards from our platoon and almost immediately thereafter got a call that the ARVN captain wanted to talk with me. I found out we had a disagreement on mounting the guards and he was unhappy with what we were doing. The ARVN practice was for two soldiers to be on guard on the dirt road in front of the camp gate. They carried their rifles at shoulder arms and marched back and forth about fifty paces in front of the gates, crossing each other's path as they went. This was a standard method in garrison that the ARVN had taken to the field. In the field, my guys were used to hiding themselves in brush-covered positions just off the road, where they could observe the gate area as well as the general vicinity in front of the camp. The captain wanted my guys to match his unit's SOP of marching up and down the road. My NCO asked me to intervene, making the point that this method would just make our guys targets for the VC if they should attack. I agreed with my NCO, but I needed something to convince the captain. The starlight scope came to my rescue. The U.S. Army had begun issuing the first night-vision devices in the mid-1960s, and my platoon had been given one for this assignment. The ARVN captain was completely unaware of the scope and its abilities. I asked the NCO to bring the scope, which was mounted on an M-14 rifle, over to me. We turned it on. It's battery was not strong enough for it to be on continuously, so it had to be turned on periodically throughout the night in order to scan the target areas. I gave it to the captain to look through. He had never seen one and was quite amazed at its ability to turn night into green-lit day. I explained that it was more effective to have my men in a concealed position, periodically scanning the front area than marching back and forth carrying this heavy device. I would learn later in my life in Asia that all that was needed was some way to save face in these situations. After hearing my explanation and inspecting the scope, the ARVN captain agreed to mount the guard in the fashion my NCO had ordered. The starlight scope was the necessary face-saver. I learned later that this device was not being shared with the ARVN forces at the time, but I felt I couldn't very well keep it a secret from the captain because we were camped with his troops.

CHAPTER 10
AIR ASSAULT

The problem with much combat training is that, no matter how realistic the military tries to make it, it doesn't *seem* real. It seems like a movie. You have no expectation of death. My training followed that pattern except for one incident at the Jungle Expert School, at Fort Amador, Panama. The occasion was the briefing session we were given prior to undertaking an escape-and-evasion course. We were a class of several hundred junior infantry officers and NCOs on our way to Vietnam. On this day, we were called to sit in a semi-circle on the shoreline just short of a wooden pier projecting ten meters into a small bay. A river flowed out of the jungle to our left, and the jungle on our right curved out toward the ocean for two hundred meters, which provided some protection from the biggest waves.

The instructor had set up a large easel with a map and had his back to the ocean as he pointed out terrain points we would encounter as we moved through the course. Midway to the open ocean, some sixty meters out, we could see three or four as they swam in a circle, their dorsal fins breaking the surface for a few seconds at a time, then submerging, and then breaking water again. It was a mesmerizing sight, a quiet, calm, understated message of menace. These waters belonged to the sharks, not to us infantry soldiers, but we were being instructed to share their home.

A battered wooden barracks structure on the near side of the river was the destination point for our escape. We would be let go in the jungle swamp behind a mountainous area on the other side of the river. Once we were through the swamp and over the mountain we had to cross the river any way we could. That crossing was essential to completion of the course. This opened up the first real bout of fear I felt in any of my military training so far. The night before my first parachute jump was a long one, but that was nerves, not real fear. It took the menace of those sharks to stir real fear. The question was, how far upriver would these ocean killers venture? In the end, my team had to swim across the brown river six hundred meters inland from the bay, and there we were more worried about alligators than sharks. Neither appeared to block the crossing.

Everyone who goes into combat remembers the first time he is shot at. That is the moment of epiphany, when you are forced to accept the reality: "Someone is trying to kill me!" Of course, it always comes as a shock. No matter how much training you have had, no matter if you have been in-country for a while and possibly seen the aftermath of a battle or a fire fight, you are initially an observer. It just seems inconceivable that someone would actually want to kill *YOU*. Then, after the event, you come to accept it because you really have no other choice. You are just another target to the opposition, those others you have come to kill. This brings a whole new level of fear to every waking moment. Before, you were scared and nervous. There were so many unknowns, so many new risks. But that fear was generalized: a chopper you were on could crash, or some clown handling his rifle incorrectly could accidentally discharge a round and hit you. But now the fear is real and personalized. They. Want. To. Kill. You. One of them actually aimed at you or in your direction and let loose gunfire. They wanted to see you go down, and if it was a kill shot, so much the better. Now you can join the club of those who wake up every morning wondering if you are going to become a target today. What if today is your last day? What is the assignment? Are you going on patrol? Are you going to take part in an air assault? If the answer is yes, the weak knees start, and the fear mounts throughout the period of preparation. If it's a night patrol, the fear builds during the combat inspection, even before you cross the wire. You fight to banish it and focus, focus, focus, on the assignment. As you go out, you look around constantly, wherever they might be waiting for you, waiting in ambush or deliberately allowing you to continue on your way out, and then ambushing you on your way back into camp the next morning.

This particular day was to start with an air assault. It was my first. We had returned to the Cu Chi base a couple of weeks after my arrival in Vietnam and were quickly tasked to go back out. Before the choppers even arrived, I had a repeat moment of decision akin to the one at Camp Alpha a few weeks earlier. The sun had been up for over an hour, but the heat of the day had not yet hit as we filed out of the base camp to a dirt road that crossed a nearby open area. We were lined up in groups of six along the dirt road, which would serve as the pick-up zone. Six was the number of combat-laden American soldiers a Huey slick ship or transport chopper could carry in the tropical heat.

As we waited for the choppers to arrive one of my squad leaders, Sergeant Bobby Wood, grabbed me by the arm and said, "Sir, when we get on the choppers, don't sit on the end seat. Get in the middle. That way you're less likely to be hit by ground fire if the LZ is hot when we come in."

I was dumbfounded. The other four soldiers in our group were all listening to see what I would say and do. I was aware that this was the first of many decisions that would define who I was as a leader with these soldiers, but I was also aware that Sergeant Wood knew what he was talking about and meant well. He sincerely didn't want to lose his new platoon leader on his first assault. I told him, "Thanks, Sergeant Wood, but I'll let one of the other guys have that seat. I'll board last."

He just shook his head and said, "Okay, sir." It was clear that he thought I should take his advice. The motto at The Infantry School at Fort Benning is "Follow Me." Furthermore, the motto of the Ranger School at Fort Benning is "Rangers Lead the Way." This concept of leading from the front gets drilled into infantry leaders during every phase of their training, and you can't lead from the safe seats!

When the choppers arrived to pick us up, I got aboard last and sat on the floor. We had four soldiers sitting on the web seats, and I and another soldier sat on the floor, back-to-back, facing the open doors. From this position, I could see everything unfold as we came in and I could be the first to jump down when the chopper reached the LZ. I noted that Sergeant Wood, despite his advice to me, sat on an end seat.

The assault force comprised two companies of infantry: Alpha, 4/9, my company, and Bravo, 4/9, flying in together. To my knowledge, there was no specific enemy force target. It was just that this area on the edge of the Mekong Delta was reputed to be part of the Viet Cong supply route that led further inland, and our presence was supposed to disrupt it. Also, there was the possibility of making contact with the enemy, so we could find and confiscate some of his supplies. A village on the intersection of a river and a major canal would be the end objective following seven to eight hours of walking and checking what we might find along the way.

Aerial assaults always start with your stomach curdling as the chopper pitches and rolls in the air wake of the gunships that led the assault and prepped the site. The grunts wait aloft to see if the LZ is hot or not. In this case, there were only a few shots taken at us on landing, and whomever had taken them had disappeared by the time we unloaded from the choppers.

I was leading the 2nd Platoon of Alpha Company as we immediately went into the zone of the absurd. We jumped into the rice paddy. That same squad leader who had warned me about which seat to take, Sergeant Bobby Wood, leapt off the chopper as it hovered three feet off the deck—and immediately dropped his M-14 into the rice paddy mud. I was trying to get the platoon out of the rice paddy and into the shelter of the forest as quickly as possible. When I turned to see Sergeant Wood bent over, groping in the muddy water, I yelled, "Sergeant Wood, it's time to move out. Let's get out of this rice paddy."

"Sir, I can't. I got to find my rifle," he shouted back. I watched him bend over and feel around in the mud. He found it in minutes and, as we weren't taking fire, we could only laugh at the anticlimax of it all. It was a funny way to start the day.

Sergeant Wood was the only member of my platoon equipped with the M-14. He had requested and received special permission to continue to carry it after the rest of the platoon was rearmed with the new and much lighter M-16. I was glad he had it. You could drop an M-14 into a rice paddy, bring it up, and start firing immediately. The delicate M-16 would be pretty much useless until you broke it down and cleaned it.

The laughter and light-hearted mood quickly disappeared as we started the long, hot walk toward our objective. We soon stepped out of the rice paddies onto narrow footpaths that weaved through coconut palms, bamboo growth, and scrub brush. Even though we were in the shade, there was no breeze and the temperature was around 95 degrees. There was no tactical formation, just a long line of more than one hundred eighty sweating infantrymen. My platoon was in the rear, walking along the footpaths, periodically stopping as the troops up front checked for possible booby traps or ambushes. Then we went lurching along again.

Four hours after landing, close to noon, we took a slightly longer break, twenty minutes or so, so the troops could crack open some C-rations and make themselves a quick, cold meal. We had no idea what security precautions the lead platoon was taking, but we heard on the grapevine that some small patrols had been sent out to the flanks to check for signs of the Viet Cong. Nothing was found.

We started to walk again, start and stop, as the lead platoon made security checks along the way. Four hours after stepping off, we got word that the vanguard was nearing the objective. We were a good two hundred meters back.

I received orders to put a squad of my platoon in place as a stay-behind ambush patrol to pick off any VC who might be following us into the village in which we would spend the night. We put our lead squad into brush-covered ambush positions and then walked through, leaving them behind.

The village itself, completely unoccupied, consisted of about thirty mud-and-bamboo huts with thatched roofs. Palm trees, tall bamboo, and brush grew everywhere. The village would have been barely visible from the air. The river lay on one side, a major canal on another, and a smaller canal bisected the village. My platoon was strung out on a dirt path alongside the small canal, which had thick bamboo and forest on the other side.

And, yes, this was the site of my "First Lesson" in Chapter 1, where a brief shootout marked my first time under fire. It certainly left an impression. Charlie had taught me not just my first but also my most important lesson about war. It bears repeating. War's about killing and surviving. Nothing more.

As a footnote, there was a strange incident not long after our brush with the VC. The deserted village had been dark and gloomy as we entered, but when the sun dropped beyond the surrounding tree line we were plunged into a world of virtually total blackness. There was no moonlight and the stars were completely hidden behind a high cloud cover. None of the men spoke or moved. The silence was oppressive. We weren't allowed to smoke because the flare of a lighter would have given any sniper waiting outside the perimeter a target to shoot at. The feeling of total isolation was so strong we might as well have been on another planet.

Then the night erupted as a red lance of fire was thrown out of the sky toward the jungle a kilometer away, across the river, followed a split-second later by an enormous, roaring cacophony. It was a dragon's fiery breath highlighted by the backdrop of the barren, black void. I was astonished.

I had never seen or heard anything like this before. I was sitting on the trail next to Sergeant Amado and asked him, "What the hell was that?" He told me it was indeed a dragon, at least the Air Force's version. It was a C-47 cargo plane converted to a ground-support gunship role for Vietnam. The Air Force had nicknamed it Puff the Magic Dragon, though the call sign was Spooky.

Puff had three super-machine guns mounted on one side, each capable of putting out a hundred rounds a second. A periodic burst of red lightning tailing off into the ground with a following roar as the sound caught up with the light show went on for more then twenty minutes. Apparently, a Vietnamese army unit was under an overwhelming attack, and the American military advisor had called for support fire. I had the very selfish thought that I was glad the other troops needed the support rather than us. Then, show over, the night shut down on us again.

A footnote to this first time I came under fire was what happened later in the evening. The VC near the village we occupied had fired and run. There was no additional contact, but we were in the Mekong Delta, so slowly throughout the evening, inch by inch, foot by foot, the water in the river and the canals rose until it was a mere twelve inches beneath the top of the plank bed my RTO and I were sitting on. The village was flooded. I doubt if anyone in our battalion or division planning staff had understood how far inland the ocean tides infiltrated the Mekong Delta.

The listening post called in at midnight to say they were sitting up to their necks in water. "What should we do?" Of course, the only answer was, "Stay in position." The water would go down; splashing about at night would only put them in danger.

This flow of what was essentially river-bottom water was the source of the stench in the village. The residue settled with the ebb and the sun baked it through the day. In the morning as the tide ebbed, the village was once again dry.

We were extracted via the river by assault landing craft manned by the South Vietnamese navy. The entire foray was an educational experience for a green lieutenant and a miserable, frustrating one for all the troops.

There is really no time to reflect in combat, but as I have looked back on that encounter over the months and years, several thoughts occurred to me. My first thought was about how much courage it took for five or six VC—farmers, really—to sneak up and ambush one hundred eighty or so heavily armed American soldiers. The second thought was just how ineptly we, the American troops, were being led in that we were essentially stumbling around unknown and inhospitable Delta rice-growing countryside, hoping somehow to inflict damage on the enemy. As with our own American Revolutionary War, the large foreign military machine often couldn't find a target on which to focus its power. This incident planted a seed of doubt in my mind about our leadership's understanding of the country we were in and the war we were fighting. That seed was to grow to fruition before I left Vietnam.

CHAPTER 11
IN GARRISON

Following several more days in the field, we were sent back to Cu Chi to clean our equipment and prepare for the next air assault. During this period, an opportunity came up for me to build my relationship with the men in my platoon.

The troops were looking forward to a break from constantly being wet and hiking through the jungle on 95-degree days, looking for Charlie. I shared that desire for a break. I knew we would be busy but thought it would be low-key activities such as cleaning weapons and possibly some practice with the M-16s, machine guns, and mortars—nothing too taxing. I was really upset, as were my troops, when we were the only platoon ordered to spend a day rebuilding the bunkers on the Cu Chi perimeter defense line near our battalion area. This consisted of taking out deteriorating sandbags, filling new bags with sand or dirt, and putting them into place. All of this was to be done under the direct sun in blazing 95-degree heat.

When we got the orders early in the morning, right after breakfast, I could hear the guys grumbling, "This is our reward for humping our asses in the boonies every day?" They were pissed off, and I didn't blame them. I walked out with the guys to the bunker line and saw them get started. The NCOs were looking at me and asked, "L.T., why are we getting this duty?"

I had no idea; maybe because I was the new guy, maybe just the luck of the draw.

I looked at how slowly the men were working. They were really dragging their asses and complaining. I couldn't blame them. I thought there was no way we would finish the job in one day. If we were back out there the next day, I would have a bunch of really angry troopers on my hands.

Then a thought occurred to me. Maybe there was a way to turn this around. I hustled back up the hillside to the company headquarters and went straight to the first sergeant. He was the senior NCO in the company; he reported directly to the company commander. He, not the company commander, was the man responsible for all the work details. I asked the first sergeant if we could make a deal. I wasn't asking out of the work assignment, but I did pose this: "If my guys can finish the bunker line work in half a day, could I get a truck to take them over to the enlisted men's club on the base so they can relax and get a beer during the afternoon?"

He looked me over for a few seconds. I'm sure he was considering the need for transportation and any other administration required, then balancing it against getting the job done correctly. He agreed. If my guys got the job done in a reasonable time, say by lunch break or soon thereafter, he would have trucks available and they could go over to the enlisted men's club and take the rest of the day off.

I ran back to the bunker line, called Platoon Sergeant Amado and the squad leaders together, and briefed them. They were surprised, but they bought into it and then turned and told the guys about the deal. "Move your asses. Let's get this done."

They hustled, got the job done by 1:30 p.m., then I had the pleasure of watching them load onto the trucks to go for a well-earned drink. I also had to worry four hours later as they returned, many drunk as skunks, and unloaded from the trucks back in the company area. Almost all of them skipped chow, stumbled into the barracks, and hit the sack. I was lucky nobody got into trouble, and I was golden with the NCOs and the guys in my platoon after that.

When I thought about it later, I came to believe what helped me out was having the experience talking with the NCOs on the training ranges at Fort Jackson. My experience on that side of the officer–enlisted divide allowed me to see the work detail from their point of view and look for an alternative way to do things. It was a great help in doing my job effectively as a rifle platoon leader. Many officers would have ignored the situation, thinking it was something for the NCOs to handle. I just couldn't. Also, I knew enough to go straight to the first sergeant and ask his help when I was looking for a solution. A lot of new officers who didn't have the OCS background might well have gone to the company commander, who I'm sure would have told them, "Don't bother me. Go see the first sergeant." I had the experience to know who ran what in the army, and it was a big help.

October 1966

The number of American military:

KIA was 342

WIA was 2,189

DOC was 137

CHAPTER 12
RIVER CROSSING

Death is always present. That is the essence of combat and life in a combat zone. It might come at the most unexpected moment or in the most unexpected way, but you must learn, you must carry the knowledge in your fiber, that death is ever-present, and you must be on the lookout for it at all times.

In normal circumstances, a river crossing need not be dangerous, though it requires great care. Even in combat zones, if you are not under fire or engaged with the enemy or under emergency time pressure, there need be no danger. This was such an occasion.

We were on an expedition that was somewhat bizarre in nature, but which those who have lived the military experience will know is possible, even if it's not completely intelligible in the clear light of normal—as opposed to war—logic.

The most prized possession a career military officer can take back with him from a combat zone is a medal for valor earned in an engagement with enemy forces or, failing that, an efficiency report that shows that he led troops in combat situations and acquitted himself well while doing so.

This qualification is a must for the career-minded infantry officer. Unfortunately, not all infantry officers assigned to combat zones fall into the rank categories needed for leadership positions at the platoon, company, or battalion levels. For example, it is lieutenants, usually second lieutenants, who receive the platoon-leader positions. Company commanders usually hold the rank of captain, with first lieutenants serving as company executive officers assisting the company commander with the administrative duties.

I should point out that not all officers of ostensibly equal rank are in fact equal in the military pecking order. The source of an officer's commission is one important indicator of future successful promotions. West Point graduates are deemed to be the best qualified overall, with their in-depth academic training as well as four years of disciplined lifestyle and military indoctrination.

As graduates, they are given priority for specialized training and ongoing related assignments, such as airborne training or Ranger School. The next category is composed of ROTC graduates. The final major category of new officers is comprised those OCS graduates who are drawn from the ranks of enlisted men recommended by their commanding officers and considered to have shown unusual promise in the performance of their duties. I was a member of this last group.

The United States Military Academy at West Point graduates one thousand new officers a year, of whom two hundred and fifty or so will go into the infantry branch, which is considered the fastest, surest road to a general's star. West Pointers are a minority of the officers commissioned into the infantry branch. Their numbers have varied over the years, but ROTC colleges provide the second largest number, one thousand or more a year for the infantry. In 1965, the year I graduated from Infantry OCS, which involved a six-month course, there were roughly one thousand two hundred infantry lieutenants commissioned through OCS, the largest source of infantry officers. My class started with two hundred twenty candidates, of whom one hundred thirty-five graduated, plus ten candidates recycled from the previous class. Later in the war, the OCS course was reduced to three months and more than seven thousand infantry OCS officers were commissioned between1967 and 1971.

Of course, once you are in combat, the source of your commission becomes irrelevant. The troops don't care, though there is a widespread sense that West Point officers are focused throughout their careers on the steps that will help them achieve their generals' stars and are just putting in time until they reach the lieutenant colonel rank and achieve battalion command, which is the main qualification for their ultimate goal. The general feeling is that junior ROTC officers are "civilians in uniform" when they come on active duty, without any understanding of how the day-to-day army functions. I found that my platoon sergeant and other NCOs were comfortable with me as an OCS officer, believing I would understand the enlisted troops' needs better and mediate some of the silly orders that routinely come down from above. Nevertheless, it's your conduct as a troop leader that matters, and the key to effective combat by the men is having competent NCOs and junior officers. That only comes from individual ability and dedication to training.

There is one other qualifier pertaining to an officer's status that indicates the likelihood of future promotion and that is the type of commission held, whether it be a regular army (RA) or a reserve commission. All West Pointers receive RA commissions on graduation, and the top class leaders in ROTC and OCS may also receive them. The remaining officers, the bulk of the junior officer corps, receive reserve commissions. Though they have the bars on their shoulders, their regular, or substantive, army rank may be non-commissioned, sergeant most likely. This the army to expand the officer corps as more officers are needed in time of war, and to shrink it back to just the RA officers as the army contracts in time of peace. After World War II, many reserve officers, some up to lieutenant colonel in rank, found themselves reduced back to their regular army rank of sergeant, a difficult experience, I would imagine.

Why is this explanation necessary? Because without it, one

may find it difficult to understand why the following escapade was even planned, much less allowed to happen.

In Alpha, 4/9, we had a first lieutenant serving as company executive officer, or XO. Let's call him Lieutenant B. He was six foot two and must have weighed 225 pounds. He looked like a football lineman. Lieutenant B was an obnoxious fellow, not liked in the company by either the enlisted men or his fellow officers. As an example, he was the kind of first lieutenant who insisted that the second lieutenants he encountered salute him. Most in the military understand that rank distinctions among lieutenants are nebulous. In my second week in the unit, when the company was back in Cu Chi, the junior officers sat talking in our hooch preparing to sack out late. Lieutenant B came in and decided to haze the new officer. He ordered me to go down to the cooks' sleeping area, wake them up, and have them make him a pizza. I was incredulous; if we were back in the States, I would have been able to understand some level of hazing, but not here in Vietnam. I made him repeat the order, said "Yes, sir," and walked down to the bunker line, sat on a sand-bagged wall and stared at the stars for a couple of hours, wondering how I could have ended up serving with such a stupid officer. I went back to the hooch, where all the other officers were sleeping by then, lay down on my cot, and forgot about it.

Lieutenant B was a West Point graduate and thus held a regular army commission, but he had come to Vietnam too senior in rank to get a rifle platoon and too junior to get a rifle company to command. This posed a serious dilemma for his career promotion prospects. Now that his tour was coming to an end, he understood that he needed time as a leader in the field to get his ticket punched with a combat efficiency report that would keep him in the competition for higher rank when he was evaluated against his peers. This peer ranking is a constant source of pressure in the career military, and any deviation from the most promising path can be a reason to fall behind your classmates in the promotion parade toward a general's star. The reality is that, once you fall behind, you can never catch up. Lieutenant B had earlier received an important career assignment out of West Point, service as a rifle platoon leader with the 82nd Airborne Division. But that unit was in the States. He didn't have a combat leadership record as yet.

Somehow, Lieutenant B made his case concerning the promotion risk he was running to our battalion commander, also a West Point grad who understood the implications of the problem. Lieutenant B's career would suffer if he was transferred to another staff job without a very positive mention of combat leadership in his Officer Efficiency Report. The solution was to manufacture a field operation. This is what enlisted men and other non-West Point officers, would call the WPPA (West Point Protective Association) at work.

The solution in this instance would be a special operation for Alpha Company alone. The company was divided into two units of two platoons each, one unit led by the company commander, Captain Neilsen—*not* a West Point grad, but an excellent soldier and leader nonetheless. The other unit was led by Lieutenant B. Unfortunately, my platoon was assigned to Lieutenant B's unit.

Both units carried out an airmobile assault on positions several kilometers apart along a narrow dirt road running along the edge of the Mekong Delta. Our captain's unit would serve as a blocking force and Lieutenant B's force was to organize after the choppers dropped us off and sweep along the road toward the captain's position, supposedly driving any VC in the area toward it. This was a standard operational format when we had intelligence about the presence of enemy forces in an area. It looked good when drawn with arrows on the plastic overlay of the battalion and brigade operations maps, and it would be presented to division command as another aggressive tactical move by the battalion. Of course, in this operation, there were no known enemy forces in the area, otherwise I doubt that the senior officers would have trusted Lieutenant B in the field.

It was the end of the rainy season. The rice paddies were

flooded, so making our way along the road was the only means we had to adhere to the script. No real tactical formation was possible.

The dirt road was twenty feet wide. The troops automatically strung out in two columns along the edges, each man putting a meter or two between himself and the man ahead of him. Up front, Lieutenant B and his RTO walked just behind the lead squad, at the point of the column. My platoon brought up the rear.

It was an extraordinarily quiet and peaceful walk. Under blue skies, the countryside setting was pristine. Green rice paddies stretched in every direction, bisected by small dikes. Off in the distance, several hundred yards away on either side of the road, were lines of palm trees and occasional clusters of other trees. Not a human being, hut, water buffalo, or machine was in sight. Herons strutted, heads bobbing down occasionally, through the water of the rice paddies. The only noise was the occasional chirping of birds. Of course, we were sure we were being observed.

The file moved along fairly smoothly, which I took to be a sign that Lieutenant B wanted to show his efficiency and close on the blocking group in good time. In as much as we presented a nice target as we crossed the rice paddies, I was happy that we kept moving, but after a couple of hours we came to an obstacle.

Running directly in front of us, more than five feet higher then the level of the road, we found the wall of a major dike. The Delta is crisscrossed with a tremendous dike system that channels the waters of the Mekong River as far as possible into the countryside, so more land can be flooded for rice farming. This flow reverses and runs back into the rivers at the end of the rainy season.

The lead elements of our column, led by Lieutenant B, climbed up the mud wall and down the other side to find the waters rushing through a canal formed by the dike walls. The word came back to us that the canal, some twenty feet in width, was full of water from recent rains and that the current was strong. We now faced a significant challenge in our countryside walk designed to improve Lieutenant B's efficiency report.

My platoon was stopped on the road as Lieutenant B organized the water crossing. I couldn't see the canal or the men working there because the dike wall blocked our vision. We could hear some talking on the other side, and an occasional shouted order from Lieutenant B, but as we waited to cross over our attention was focused on the tree lines on either side of the road, looking for signs of enemy activity.

The silence was suddenly broken by loud, incoherent yells, which then turned to screams, but the noise moved rapidly away, farther down the canal. After a minute or two, which seemed like hours, the screaming stopped and all went quiet. Those of us still waiting to cross shouted towards the point of the column to ask what the hell was going on. The word came back that the dugout canoe they were using to ferry two soldiers across at a time had turned over. The soldiers, who were from the lead platoon, were wearing all their web gear as well as their helmets.

The two soldiers were swept away and dragged under by the current. They were gone. We were all in shock. How the hell could this happen? We were neither under fire nor under any time pressure at all that I was aware of. How could the water crossing be so messed up that we had lost two soldiers?

My platoon waited for our turn to be called to climb the wall of the dike and descend to cross the canal. Lieutenant B was now on the other side, so I took a second to ask one of the troopers handling the crossing ropes what had happened. He told me that Lieutenant B had ordered the soldiers to keep their web gear on, with ammo pouches, hand grenades, and other heavy items strapped to it so they would be "combat ready," as Lieutenant B put it, when they reached the other side. Also, although there was a guide rope for the dugout strung across the canal, no safety rope had been provided downstream for soldiers to catch onto in case they fell into the water.

Now that the danger had been highlighted with the loss of the two men, soldiers were taking off their web gear and holding it in one hand as they sat in the dugout to make the short crossing, and there was now a safety rope strung across the canal thirty feet below the crossing point. Lieutenant B's deluded notion of being combat ready in this situation had just killed two men.

My platoon safely made the crossing and the unit, under Lieutenant B's direction, continued its combat sweep down the road.

It was an extremely quiet group of men. We were all in shock. The stupidity and suddenness of the deaths of the two men had shaken us. There was nothing to say.

Lieutenant B had radioed in to the company commander his report of the crossing and the loss of the two men. I believe that was the reason it was decided to bring our day's walk to an end. We came to an area with a dry, elevated field suitable for a helicopter pick-up zone. Our unit was ordered to stop there and wait to be extracted by the choppers.

Lieutenant B hustled to the site, where he arranged the troops in six-man groupings to match up with each chopper as it landed, but he had one more tragicomic performance up his sleeve.

It is normal practice for troops on the ground who guided in choppers to throw a smoke grenade—"pop smoke"—at one end of the landing zone. This smoke and its color (purple, red, yellow, and so on) identified the landing zone for the chopper pilots and also provided them with the wind direction as they swept in to touch down for the troops to jump aboard. As we looked on, I was standing within earshot of Lieutenant B's RTO as B prepared the landing zone for the choppers by popping smoke. But for some reason he threw not just one smoke grenade at the head point of the landing zone, he then raced around the grid throwing more down on each side and at the other end. The landing zone was now more like the Twilight Zone, with multicolored smoke swirling in all directions.

The cursing over the radio from the leader of the chopper flight was magnificent in its originality and venom. There was no way he was bringing his flight in to land in the swirling, smoky haze Lieutenant B had created. He led a go-around as he waited for the haze to clear, meanwhile asking Lieutenant B what the hell he thought he was doing. Lieutenant B answered "I was marking all sides of the zone for you." This was an answer so incredible in its stupidity that the flight leader was silenced. He said nothing for a few seconds and then, as the smoke and haze cleared, called down "We're coming in now." Of course, we can be sure that he relayed the whole incident later to our battalion commander in the most vivid of terms. Nothing would compensate for the loss of our two men, but as I sat in the chopper taking me back to base camp I was comforted by the belief that Lieutenant B's career was surely pretty much over. I wasn't certain what he would end up doing, but, if there was a God in heaven, he would never be given the chance to lead men in the field again.

About three days later, we got word that the bodies of our two missing men had been recovered thanks to a South Vietnamese Army unit patrolling the river. The bodies had become entangled in the lower branches of the mangrove trees growing along the banks of the river the water rerouted by the big dike flowed into.

I had no idea how the tremendously powerful and untrustworthy public relations program of the U.S. Army would describe their deaths to the families, but they would be listed as non-combat casualties, which can amount to as much as one-sixth of the men lost in any of our military adventures. Almost without exception, some form of leadership incompetence caused these deaths. That is a fact the U.S. military public relations machine finds inconvenient to share with the public. For me, it started a personal campaign to ensure that neither I nor the men I led would die of stupidity, be it ours or that of others.

I have never forgotten that initial surprised and panic-stricken yelling and then the terrified screaming for help as those two young men were swept down the canal, dragged underwater by their saturated web gear, and then bobbing up to scream again once or twice, understanding they were doomed. I could envision them desperately clutching at the slick mud walls of the canal. Then, the even greater shock, the absence of noise, the terrible silence as they disappeared beneath the rushing dark brown water for good. They deserved so much better from their leaders, but I doubt the army PR machine let their families know the actual facts, as they joined the other 135 non-combat deaths recorded by the military in Vietnam that October. The psychological trauma of hearing the desperate cries of these men and, for their few buddies standing within the canal walls, witnessing their friends being swept away, was the kind of wound that would never heal for those of us at the scene.

Breaking camp. Long An province, December 1966.

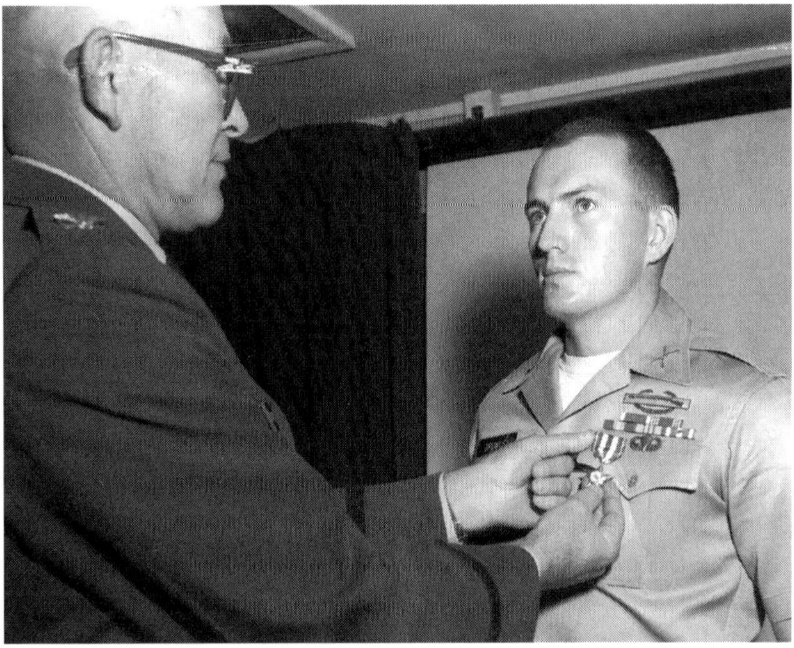

Award of Silver Star. Camp Zama army hospital, Japan, February 1967.

My hooch while I was a staff officer, Long An province, March 1967.

Moving with the battalion from Cu Chi to Fire Support Base Martha, April 1967.

Manning the battalion tactical operations centre radio. Fire support base Martha, Hau Nghia province, May 1967.

Chi at his desk as a Major leading what his family termed an "Anti-communist Tiger Force", Dat Do Province, 1973.

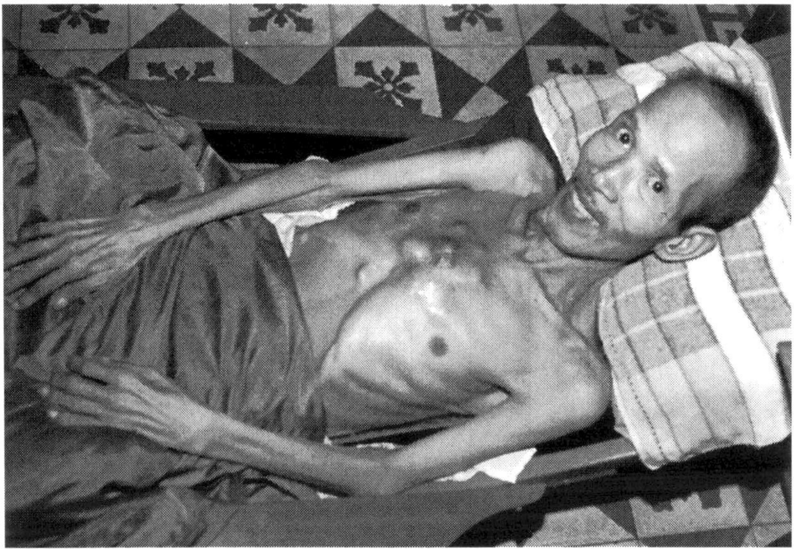

Chi as the communists delivered him home to his family. Saigon, November 1987.

November 1966

The number of American military:

KIA was 356

WIA was 2,998.

DOC was 149

CHAPTER 13
DEAD MAN WALKING

There can come a point in combat, for those whose job it is to go out where you know hat people will be trying to kill you, when as soon as you get the orders and know that your turn has come again, you start to be paralyzed with fear. It can be after involvement in a few fire fights or after a few months of action, but normally it's not too long after your first shootout. This can happen to anyone, and everybody has to fight to accommodate his fear and get on with the job. Those who don't become the subject of scorn, possibly sympathetic, but scorn nonetheless. Just another "chicken bastard," someone will say, as one platoon leader in my battalion was tagged, and they'll be right.

Another aspect of this is the phenomenon among combat troops is that, one day, a soldier will wake with the sure knowledge that it's his day to die. There are accounts of soldiers insisting on giving their best buddies mementos they had been carrying, possibly for months, or something brought along from home. There are stories of soldiers writing a last note home and giving it to a buddy, asking him to mail it if the soldier didn't survive the day.

My moment came when I had been in-country for about two months. During that time, we had only been in one shootout of any real scale and came through with no casualties. There had been a few quick brushes with VC groups and some sniper rounds coming our way since then, and we were mortared in the field at one point, but my platoon had sustained no serious injuries. No one had been killed in action.

On this occasion, we had actually left the field and gone back to the division base camp, which brought feelings of relative safety in that, except for a few mortar rounds coming in, there was no reason to expect serious enemy activity. Then, late one afternoon, I was notified that my platoon had been selected for an ambush patrol the next day.

It was normal to send out patrols around the division base camp to ensure that the VC couldn't bring mortar units within a thousand or so meters and shell the camp. A perimeter of around three hundred meters had been cleared all around the camp to provide fields of fire in case of attack. Two sides of the Cu Chi camp, on the north and the east, were fronted by the Filhol rubber plantation. These rubber trees were a residue of the French colonial occupation. My patrol was to hike out from a heavily sandbagged outpost on the edge of the camp perimeter known as Ann-Margret. It was named after the movie star who had visited the camp and that outpost earlier in the year on a USO tour.

The plan was simple; we would walk northeast the three hundred meters through the open area until we reached the tree line. We would penetrate the trees a further two hundred meters, so we could be confident our patrol was not being directly observed by VC watchers. Once we were deep inside the plantation, we were to make a sharp break to the right and head to a trail that cut through the plantation area directly east of the camp, then set up an ambush position before dark.

This last instruction highlights the very unusual nature of this patrol. We normally left whatever base we occupied to go on patrol just after the sun set. Operating in the dark kept enemy observers from knowing just how many soldiers might be coming out and what direction they would take. This idea of going out in full daylight, when Charlie would be watching and counting us, concerned me. I didn't like it and I knew the troops wouldn't like it.

In the morning, I went over to the battalion operations center to get the patrol orders. I was able to go over the route and plan with the battalion operations officer, the S3, a major. I had done this in one form or another many times before and handled my nerves well, but for some reason I was sick with apprehension that day. I was shocked at my fear. I had awakened feeling as if I was doomed, and I couldn't shake the sensation. This premonition was strong and grew stronger throughout the day.

Back at my tent, I called a meeting with the two squad leaders who would be going out with me and briefed them. In addition to myself , my RTO, and our medic, the total number on the patrol would be twenty men taken from their two squads rather, than the full platoon of forty. Trucks would come for us at 2:00 p.m. and take us to Ann-Margret, where we would walk out through the wire surrounding the division base camp. We would inspect the troops and their gear and prepare to leave the outpost at 3:00 p.m. All was in order.

My fear continued to grow as we boarded the trucks. When we reached the outpost, I barely had the strength to climb down off the truck. The day seemed to match my mood; it was as hot as usual but overcast, and the air felt heavy and gloomy. I was wondering if my fear was showing as I inspected the men, their weapons, and gear before we set out. I could normally make a joke or two to try to relax the men I was leading. I was speechless this day, and so scared that I wanted to puke, but I couldn't.

Following the inspection, I just turned to the squad leader whose men were taking point, indicated the compass direction we wanted to follow, and told him to lead us out. My fear grew as we zigzagged our way through the wire. I felt as if I was going to my death, and I didn't want to die.

The physical act of walking didn't calm me down, but it did allow me to think a bit. My mind was swirling during that three-hundred meter walk to the tree line. I was thinking about how I didn't want to disgrace my family or let my men down. At the same time, I thought about how much I didn't want to die. I was thinking about the life I had yet to live.

Each step felt like it was carrying me closer to death. In my mind, I was a dead man walking.

The fact that my men and squad leaders were all experienced meant that there was no talking as we made our way out. Perhaps many were having the same thoughts I was having or, knowing what a good target we made as we emerged into the open, were just super-focused on the area around us. The silence helped me greatly as I wrestled with my fear.

Somehow, while traversing those three hundred meters of clear ground, I found resolution. It came to me that there were things worse than death, and that I had to cling to that thought. I reached a place of acceptance. I was dead. I was dead and should accept it and get on with my job.

I was going to die. If not today, then on another patrol or air assault in the future. That had to be okay. When I accepted that I was dead, I was able to come to terms with the needs of the day. Not that I lost my desire to live. As we entered the tree line, I was more intensely focused on our surroundings than before. Somehow, I knew, I could do my job, because I had accepted the worst that could happen.

I don't know in detail how other men handle that fear of death or a premonition as strong as I experienced, but I am sure that, over thousands of years, many have walked down that same emotional path that I had just traveled and come to the same conclusion: accept death and get on with the job. In retrospect, I don't see how it could be done otherwise, and that was my route.

Once we had passed the tree line and had traveled a further two hundred meters or so, I passed the word to stop, then went forward to talk with the point squad leader. As we were getting closer to the ambush area and I had ceased to be so absorbed with myself, I could now sense the tension that was building in the patrol. I gave the squad leader the new compass direction through the trees of the rubber plantation, and we headed out.

At that time, I had no knowledge of rubber trees or rubber plantations though I would become very familiar with them over the passing years while living later in Malaysia and Thailand. Actually, a walk through a rubber plantation can be a lovely experience. The trees are not large, possibly twelve to fourteen inches in diameter and twenty or so feet high. They are evenly spaced about ten feet apart and run in straight ranks for hundreds of meters, so that you can see between the rows quite a distance ahead and to your left and right as you walk along. The sunlight, weak this day, provided patches of illumination between the dark spaces in the shade of the foliage, and the overall effect was of a series of connected, dimly lit tunnels. There was not a sound. No birds singing. Nothing. The ground was moist and soft underfoot as the rainy season had recently ended, so the footsteps of the troops as they walked along were muffled.

The tension continued to rise as we walked further into the rubber plantation, the men half-crouched now, prepared to hit the ground and start firing at the first sign that Charlie was in the neighborhood. I had moved a bit farther up the line, So I could be sure that we were on the right compass heading without yelling or making any noise. I could see the point man about fifteen meters in front, and the squad leader occasionally looked back to me so I could guide him along with hands signals. A bit to the right, a bit to the left, or straight on.

Part of being a leader in *any* setting is having a mastery of the required skills. For some reason, I had always been the top of my military classes when it came to map and compass work. This was an extremely important skill for infantry leaders in Vietnam. I had no doubt I would get us to the point on the map we had been ordered to reach.

We had been out a little over two hours when, despite my

confidence, I began to be afraid that we had gotten off course. But then the point man finally stopped and turned to wave his squad leader up. After a minute or two, the squad leader turned to wave me up as well.

I told my RTO to stay in place and went to the front. We had come to the dirt trail on which we were supposed to set up the ambush and spend the night.

The point man went forward and carefully looked up and down the trail, studying it intricately. When he returned, he told us he had found a set of bicycle tracks, fresh and deeply etched into the somewhat muddy trail. The VC used bicycles as mini-trucks, loading them down with heavy ammunition or one-hundred or two-hundred pound rice bags and walking the bikes along. This seemed to be the case here.

The question was what to do next. This was the trail we had been sent out to find, and the fresh bicycle tracks indicated that the VC were using it to transport supplies, so it showed promise. If we set up the ambush here, we would have a good chance of surprising them if they came along during the night or early morning. But, it was still light out. The shadows of the trees were growing longer, but it was only a little after 5:00 p.m., and I estimated that we had a good thirty to forty-five minutes before dark.

I decided that it would be foolish to set the men in ambush positions right there and take a chance on that the VC would spot us before nightfall. I told the squad leader that we should follow the trail further toward the small deserted village shown on our map and see what we could find. If we didn't find anything in twenty minutes, we could double back through the plantation and set up the ambush along the trail after dark.

If I had thought the men were alert as we walked through the rubber plantation, the effect of reaching the trail and getting the word about the fresh bicycle tracks took the tension. Their collective demeanor rose to a whole new level. I could see it in their eyes. Of course there was fear there, but that, under control, was a good thing. I could see several men setting their M-16s on automatic, and so did I.

We set off, two abreast, on either side of the narrow trail, ready to drop into the bordering brush if necessary. The point man was leading with a shotgun in hand, and another soldier with an M-16 was walking across from him. The squad leader came next, then two more soldiers, and then me with my RTO right behind me. I was a bit further up front than The Book said I should be, but I felt I had to be able to see what came up, as the time for hand signals and waving troops around could be minimal if we came across any VC.

It was only a five-minute walk to an opening in the trail that was within sight of the first thatch-roof hut. Off to the left of the opening, we saw a stack of sharp stakes, which had been prepared for use in punji pits, the camouflaged holes the VC dug for U.S. soldiers to fall into and impale themselves on the sharpened stakes.

This was surely Charlie's home. It was originally a farm village that the VC had turned into their camp. As we took several steps toward the hut, we could see what the U.S. military would call "stacked arms" in front of it—five or six rifles leaning up against one another, butts on the ground and barrels pointing upward. We could hear the sing-song cadence of Vietnamese voices coming from inside the hut. We had caught Charlie taking his dinner break.

Being with experienced troops is everything in combat. As we entered the small clearing, I pulled up even with the squad leader and point men. Without my having to say a word, the troops behind us approached and moved to either side of us, forming a line facing the hut. Now we could see, through the trees behind the first hut. Several other huts were spread out in the small camp. I registered that there were many more VC around than the five or six men in the hut, but that thought was interrupted by a sudden silence.

The VC inside had stopped talking. They must have heard

something.

The squad leader motioned our machine gunner, Spec. 4 Bill Cline, up front to join the line facing the hut, but I had heard nothing. It didn't matter.

In a few seconds the VC came running out of the hut, all reaching for the rifles they had stacked outside the door while they ate. The point squad leader barked at the machine gunner to get them, but he didn't have to say a thing. Cline had been in Vietnam for over eight months and knew what to do. He was Rambo years before that name became known. He held his M-60 machine gun against his hip with his left hand on top of it to keep the barrel from running up as he fired. He calmly and coolly opened fire, swept back and forth across the group of VC and gunned them all down. You can say they never had a chance, and any combat soldier will tell you that's a good thing. Never give the enemy a chance. That only puts you and your buddies in danger.

There were a few seconds of silence after Cline stopped firing. I had just started to think "What do we do now?" when the VC answered for me: we started taking fire from further inside the camp.

Almost immediately, off to my right, a tree seemed to explode about twelve feet above the ground. I found out later that the other squad leader, Staff Sergeant Johnson, had spotted a VC lookout in the tree and for whatever reason had taken out a LAW anti-tank missile he carried and fired it at the man. If it had hit the VC I doubted it would have exploded; it would have gone through him. As it was, it seemed to have hit the tree and exploded, killing him.

The explosion just lent emphasis to my decision. Going into the camp and taking fire from every direction didn't seem like a smart thing to do.

I noticed that the trail led off to my right, passing just outside the camp. I called to the men to move off in that direction, remain outside, and fire into the camp.

The point man and another soldier headed down the trail in front of me. After ten paces or so, we came to a trench we had to jump over. Just before I jumped, I saw a VC about twenty feet up the trenchline stand up and raise his weapon in my direction. Before I could react, one of my men, possibly several in file behind me, shot him down.

At this point, there was so much shooting going on it was hard to know who was firing at what, but I was again thankful I was with an experienced group of soldiers. They knew what to do when Charlie was present: shoot, shoot, and shoot again. And no time for questions.

We had moved some fifty to sixty feet along the trail and were approaching the other side of the camp. There was a relatively dry rice paddy ahead, with an embankment or small dike running parallel to the village. I thought that would be a good place to put the troops in position to take the VC in the camp under fire.

Moving troops under fire is difficult, especially when you are moving away from it. It's easy for panic to set in. I stopped and stepped off the trail to try to organize the move better, because our movement along the path had turned into a rush. I knew we had to keep fire on the VC. If we all ran to cover with no one firing back, we would be a great target. With my RTO standing next to me, I touched each soldier as he went by, telling them to slow down and keep an eye over his shoulder.

After two or three men had passed, there was a tremendous explosion just off to my right. I was picked up and thrown ten to twelve feet through the air before hitting the ground. I thought I was dead. I remember thinking as I flew through the air in what seemed to be slow motion, "Now I'm going to meet God." Then I hit the ground.

I was back to reality. Amazingly, I still had my M-16 in my right hand.

As I stood up, I heard a horrible screaming.

It was my RTO. He hadn't been blown off his feet; I had taken most of the blast but he had taken several pieces of shrapnel in his legs, one of which had nicked his scrotum. He was going into shock screaming, "They've shot off my balls. They've shot off my balls." I was in a bit of a shocked state myself, but I told him to "Shut the fuck up. We'll get the medic to look at it."

The troops from further back in the file were still charging along the trail. I pushed my RTO onto the trail and told him to move along. I counted several more soldiers, and then one of them told me he was the last man.

As I backed onto the trail and then out into the clearing, toward the dike, I fired short bursts back into the camp. I had to change the magazine along the way, and just threw the used one in the dirt, not wanting to take the time to carefully stow it back in the ammo pouch.

I turned when I was halfway across the field and yelled at my RTO that I needed the radio. He shouted back that it had been hit by shrapnel and wasn't working.

Now I was closing on the dike, conscious that my men were down in position, firing back into the camp, and that we were taking fire from it. I called out that I needed the damn artillery radio if my battalion radio wasn't working. I was moving a bit slower now as I had taken shrapnel all up my right side—leg, arm, and head.

I had just finished off another magazine when one of the squad leaders emerged from behind the dike and helped me into place. Another brought the radio over. The medic came over to look at my wounds and I asked him about my RTO. He told me he would be okay. The shrapnel had just nicked his scrotum. He had bled a bit but was still serviceable, in the medic's opinion. There were five other guys with wounds, none serious.

While the medic bandaged me up, I was able to get through to the battalion operations center on the radio and let them know our situation, that we had seven wounded and were up against a possible platoon of VC, maybe twenty or thirty in number, and taking automatic weapons fire. After giving them our position, which was on the other side of the camp from where we initially intended to set up the ambush, they linked me up with an artillery battery and I was able to start calling in artillery fire on the camp area. The battalion CO told me they would dispatch a mechanized infantry company to relieve us, but that it would take several hours or more in the dark.

At one point, the S3 asked if I wanted a medevac chopper to lift out the wounded. I told him no. Having a chopper land after dark in the open field between the two sides shooting at each other would just pose an unnecessary danger to the chopper crew and those waving it in to conduct the evacuation. I had been told I had sustained the worst wounds, so I had no reservations in making the decision not to lay on the medevac.

The rest became increasingly hazy as, over the next several hours, blood loss and shock set in. At last, I told the artillery to check fire, and I gave up the radio to one of my squad leaders at about 10:30 that night, as soon as we saw the armored personnel carriers (APCs) coming into sight.

I passed out as soon as I was loaded into an APC. An hour or so later, I came to as they carried me out of the APC into the division hospital surgery room and put me on a table for the docs to work on. My battalion CO came over and told me he was proud of us, that we had done a good job. I remember telling him that I thought we had fucked up as it was such a crazy shootout. Then I passed out again.

It hadn't been my day to die after all.

In the following months, I went on airmobile assaults and night ambush patrols, and was shot at again multiple times. On one occasion, I even came under 105mm howitzer fire from an ARVN unit that didn't know my company was in the same zone they were bombarding with what we called H&I fire, which stands for "harassment and interdiction fire." It was one of the most terrifying experiences of my life, hugging the ground, trying to claw further into the soil, while listening to those shells whistle in and then explode as the ground trembled and trees splintered overhead. But I never again had the premonition and fear that I had the day I led the patrol out to the Filhol rubber plantation. I am convinced there is something in the subconscious beyond the physical realm that I had plugged in to and that many, many other combat soldiers have experienced over the years. I have no explanation except to say that it's real.

I was fortunate. I had come away alive. Many, maybe most, don't.

There was one other thought I had about that patrol as the months went by. As much as I was critical of the tactical planning we labored under on a regular basis, this was one time someone in the operations shop had got it right. There is no doubt Charlie saw us coming out from the base camp that afternoon, but once we had turned into the woods Charlie couldn't be sure just where we were going and, as communications constituted one of his weaknesses, couldn't hear from other units if they had correctly guessed. By taking a wide semi-circular route, we had essentially come in through the back door of the VC camp, arriving both at a time and from a direction they didn't expect. The edge of surprise that gave us plus the coolness of the experienced troops I was leading resulted in our being able to hurt Charlie badly and get away relatively unscathed. Even though I was unhappy about it in the beginning, it was a damn good plan.

One of the great weaknesses we had in Vietnam, at least in my experience, was that we seldom took time to conduct after-battle analysis on a small-unit level, such as platoon, company, or even battalion. My being wounded and evacuated precluded it this time, but on virtually all other occasions we seemed to be too dang busy to stop and analyze what had worked and what hadn't. One of Charlie's strengths, probably related to keeping leaders on line for years on end in his thirty-year war, was that he did just that: analyzed everything.

Most of the top generals in the U.S. military shifted in and out, getting their career tickets punched. Thus, they were too busy, too disengaged while trying to repeat their experience of World War II. Marine Corps General Lewis Walt was a significant and laudable exception to that rule.

Hindsight is always twenty/twenty, but when I read of Walt's concept of fighting the "other war" years later, I thought, "This is it. This guy had it right." General Walt was in charge of the Marine forces in the I Corps region, along South Vietnam's northern border, from mid-1965 to mid-1967. He and his staff initiated a program he called the Combined Action Company (CAC). The program sent squads of Marine volunteers into the countryside to assist local part-time South Vietnamese militias, known as Regional Forces and Popular Forces. His CAC units all had the same orders: help protect the villages, get to know the people, find the local Communist infrastructure and put it out of business. He stressed the importance of winning the confidence of ordinary Vietnamese citizens by assisting in local development projects, such as building homes and schools, by gaining trust.

Unfortunately General William Westmoreland, the big boss in Vietnam, preferred to slug it out with the VC and NVA in the style he knew from World War II. He overruled General Walt and continued to plead with Washington for more divisions, and he planned for larger set-piece battles, which were all he understood. Review of what might work and changes in approach were out of the question with the military leadership in Saigon. There was no possible "other war," there was only the slugfest.

The Viet Cong constantly reviewed what succeeded in the jungle against the clumsy American war machine, and what failed. They had failures on many occasions, but they seldom repeated them. Their reaction to the fighting above ground in the Cu Chi area was to go below ground with their camps over the following years, leading to the famous tunnels of the same name. Many of these tunnels were already in existence to a significant extent when the 25th Infantry Division first arrived on the scene, but they were all substantially expanded following the division's arrival as it became too dangerous for Charlie to show himself above ground.

In fact, the VC and NVA troops went increasingly underground all over Vietnam in order to to avoid American air power and artillery, and the long-term effect was to turn their opponent's strength into a weakness. You can't hit what you can't see.

CHAPTER 14
VUNG TAU

The transition from being in the field in a combat situation—with all my senses stretched to the fullest, looking for any sign of the enemy, and living with the tension of needing to be ready to protect myself at every moment—to lying on a hospital bed with no responsibility other than to allow trained medical people to care for me was delightfully mind-boggling. Clean sheets, decent food, some pleasant pain-killing drugs, attentive nurses, all represented heaven on earth. I had emerged alive and hadn't lost any limbs or, to my knowledge at the time, damaged my senses. I felt I had come out ahead this time.

After surgery in the hospital in Cu Chi to extract most of the shrapnel from my body, I spent the night and most of the next day there. The shrapnel was all on my right side: leg, hip, chest, arm, and head, a couple of dozen pieces in all. All were small fragments of metal from a Chinese hand grenade that the VC used. That was an important fact. An American hand grenade, an M-26, would have blown my foot off and probably killed me. The difference is in the speed of the explosive used in the grenade. The Chinese used a slower-burning explosive, which gave their weapon a more concussive heaving effect. The American version, with much higher-speed explosive material, has more of a cutting effect. I knew this from when I had been an instructor on a hand grenade training range. The cutting power of the American grenade would have sliced off my lower leg. I was lucky I still had my foot, lucky to be alive.

As evening fell, I was put on a stretcher, carried out to a Chinook helicopter, and transferred with a group of other soldiers on stretchers down to the 36th Evacuation Hospital in Vung Tau, a beach resort city south of Saigon. I had been given some drugs, so the flight felt like a fantasy. I was in the top rack of stretchers that were stacked three-deep, staring at the ceiling of the chopper. I could feel the vibrations and the rush of cool night air, and I listened to some of the guys moaning in pain. The magic of the drugs applied by the medics worked, and I dozed off. I was barely awake when the chopper landed and I was carried to a hospital bed.

I awoke the next morning in the officers' ward of the hospital. Not that there was any difference from the enlisted men's ward. It was just another exercise of the military preference for keeping officers and enlisted men apart. Neither unit had air conditioning, just screening over the open windows and fans to provide a breeze and cool the tropical air a little.

As I woke up, I surveyed the room. Most of the beds were full and most cases were more serious than mine. In the bed on my left was an Australian Army major who had been wounded in a mortar attack on his position. His shrapnel wounds were less numerous than mine but more damaging. He hadn't lost any limbs and seemed to be well on the mend. I talked with him a bit and found that he was quite depressed. The mortar attack that wounded him had killed his batman. This is a position unique to the Commonwealth nations, in which an NCO is assigned to a field-grade officer to help him pitch his tent, get his meals, and carry out other field chores in order to allow the officer more time to focus on his duties. The major and his batman had been together for several years, so the death was taking a toll on him.

Across the aisle from my bed was an ARVN officer whose

right leg was elevated somewhat. He had a gaping open wound in his lower leg caused by a bullet that had entered from the front and hit the shin bone about eight inches below the knee. Just from the nature of the wound you knew he was a brave man. That wound came from moving toward the enemy, not away. The nature of the injury and the resultant surgery to take the bullet out had left a yawning hole in his shin that had to heal from the inside out to prevent infection. In as much as the wound was open to the air to promote healing, the doctors had put a small cage over it to keep it from contact with anything that might contaminate it. This didn't prevent flies from seeking out the wound, so my strongest image of him was of his holding a fly swatter and periodically swiping them away. Another vivid memory was that he was constantly smiling and joking. This was a positive and strong-willed man. We talked across the aisle, each asking the other how he had been wounded, which unit he belonged to, and questions about our families.

His name was Luong Dinh Chi. In the Vietnamese fashion, the family name is used first, thus he was Captain Luong, but, adapting to the American fashion he told me to call him Chi. My positive impression of him was reinforced a few days after I arrived at the hospital, when a U.S. Army sergeant who was assigned to his unit as an advisor visited him. He spoke with the captain for a while and then came over to talk to me after Chi had told him I was a new friend. The sergeant was effusive in his praise of Captain Luong.

He told me that the captain was the military district chief of Dat Do Province, which was on the ocean just north of Vung Tau. While many U.S. military advisors to the ARVN complained that it was difficult to get ARVN officers to order attacks on VC units, this sergeant said it was a different story with Captain Luong. He said their biggest problem was to hold him back. He was a natural military leader who insisted on attacking when the opportunity came and was always in front of his men, leading the way. This was the third time he had been wounded. The sergeant said the men in Captain Luong's district force worshipped him both for his courage and because of his care for them.

Chi had been born in North Vietnam, but his family were Catholics and thus had been forced to flee south with nearly half a million others Catholics, when the country was divided following the Geneva Peace Accords of 1954. The communists had taken over the North and had immediately begun a process of religious and racial persecution aimed at Catholics and Chinese-derived families. Many of the refugees from the North who had fled to the South had taken up government and military positions in the Republic of Vietnam. It was clear that they were strongly anti-communist and dedicated to the fight against the occupation of the South by the northern forces.

Having the opportunity to meet and befriend Chi was a very positive outcome of my unplanned trip to the hospital. I had heard a lot of negative descriptions of the ARVN, so it was good for me to learn that they had their share of real combat leaders.

A beach resort area, Vung Tau was used by the American. military as a site for soldiers to take in-country rest and recreation (R&R). It was a pleasant setting, where soldiers could spend three days away from their duties. It was just a twenty-minute chopper ride from Cu Chi to Saigon and the same again from Saigon to Vung Tau. It was not a difficult connection at all, so the 25th Infantry Division gave soldiers who were performing well three-day passes to travel down and relax there. I was thus lucky enough to have two guys from my platoon fly down to Vung Tau on R&R and visit me while I was in hospital.

Having authority over soldiers and gaining their respect are two different things. As an officer, you are given the authority, but respect has to be earned. The troops are very fair and very clear in their judgment. For me, the fact that these two soldiers took some precious time out from their R&R to stop by, give me an update on the platoon, and wish me well meant everything.

The battalion CO might tell me I was doing a good job, but it meant a lot more when the troops did. The reality was that the entire patrol had done a good job. The fact that many of those men had been in-country for eight months and reacted immediately when the shooting started is what made all the difference.

My visitors told me that the mechanized rifle company that had relieved us along with an ARVN unit had swept the village the next day. They found seven fresh graves and blood trails leaving the site. That would be important to the battalion commander. The U.S. military reporting system valued body count highly. In my view, the important thing was that we had done our job and none of my men had been killed.

The week I spent in the hospital passed quickly. My wounds were stitched up, and as the days went by to allow some healing before I returned to my unit, I found myself anxious to get going. Besides my talks with Chi and the Australian major there was one episode that broke the boredom. I was not an ardent baseball fan, but I knew who the big boys were, and one of the greats came walking down the aisle one day to say hello. The player was Stan "The Man" Musial of the St. Louis Cardinals. He was at the end of his career, but he looked to be in great shape, at least 6 feet 2 inches tall and with very muscular arms and large hands. As he came down the aisle saying hi to the troops, I could see he was a bit uncertain about how to address all the wounded guys, but he had a big smile and a hello for each of us. He approached me from my right side and reached out to shake my hand. My right arm was not yet mobile, so I had to cross my left hand over my body to grip his. He paused for just a second and I could see the concern on his face, but then he smiled and wished me luck and moved along.

***

Finally, after a week, I was able to convince the docs that I should be released back to duty, though they said something about staying in base camp for a further week after I got back. I told them sure, but in my mind I was confident I could heal faster than that. Somehow all the fears and doubts that had plagued me the day of the patrol had lifted. There is something about young guys (I was twenty-two at the time) and their ability to bounce back from trauma. I think the reason wars are fought by the young is that only they have the ability to recover quickly from adrenalin-filled highs that leave the body feeling completely depleted of energy.

I wasn't eager to get shot at again. I was just eager to be back with my platoon. That was where I belonged.

The check-out procedure was simple. They had me sign some papers, then gave me a small amount of military currency and a one-page set of orders to get me back to my unit. It was up to me to walk out to the chopper pad and find a lift up to Camp Alpha at Tan Son Nhut Air Base and onwards to Cu Chi. Before I left I said goodbye to the guys in the beds nearest me and then walked across to shake hands with Chi. I could tell he was dying of boredom. This was a man committed to action but forced to accept the long, slow healing process of the wound in his leg. As I extended my hand, he did something that would eventually carry great import. He wanted us to stay in touch and he gave me a three-by-five card, so common then but seldom used anymore, with his home address in Saigon. On the back he wrote, "Please don't forget. Write us." I promised I would remember and tucked the card away in my uniform.

As I walked out toward the chopper pad, I had a thought. It was early afternoon and, since we were close to the coast and I would be spending the night in Camp Alpha anyway, why not hitch a ride down to the beach and spend a few minutes looking at the ocean? My idea was to have just a small bit of tourism and relaxation prior to getting on the chopper.

There was no civilian transportation in the area; we were outside the city proper. Nevertheless, there were army trucks and jeeps coming and going. No one would ask any questions. Just stick out a hand and wave, and a truck would stop. So I walked off the hospital area, waved for a while, and sure enough a truck stopped and the driver asked where I wanted to go. I told him I wanted to see the beach area. He said "No problem, Lieutenant." I jumped in, and ten minutes later he dropped me off at a traffic circle where the main road ran along the beach and a second road ran off the circle at a ninety-degree angle, inland. It was a medium-hot day for Vietnam, about 90 degrees Fahrenheit, with clear blue skies.

I didn't think I was up to walking on the beach, but there was a stand just off the circle, possibly a bus stop, with a bench and a cover providing shade. I walked over to it and just sat on the bench and relaxed, taking in the beach and the ocean. The area along the road was not built up and there were almost no people on the section of beach in front of me. It was an off-white sandy stretch about sixty feet from a short roadside seawall down to the water. I had been to Hilton Head Island in Georgia the previous summer, which was spectacular, so I now found this section of the South China Sea disappointing. There were no waves to speak of, just an eight-to-twelve-inch ripple of water coming ashore. The color of the water was darker than the deep blue of the Atlantic, influenced by the muddy brown outpouring of the Saigon River a few miles away. It was not something to write home about.

The area across from the beach was pretty much empty. Looking around, I spotted a Coca-Cola sign on a stand across the road that led away from the beach and decided to walk over to get a Coke and do my beach-watching from there.

The thatch-roof stand was simple: cinderblock walls on two sides, and open on the other two to let in the breeze from the ocean. There were seven or eight round metal tables and chairs, and a small bar and refrigerator in the back.

There were no other customers, so I picked a table in the front from which I could have a good view of the ocean and I sat down. I was still not moving very fast, and it was good to sit after my short walk.

There was a group of young Vietnamese girls sitting around two tables in the back. My thought was that they were just out to meet each other and enjoy the ocean breeze as I was doing. They were all dressed in the Vietnamese women's national costume, the ao dai. This consists of billowy white trousers, covered by a top that serves as a form-fitting blouse that extends down to the ankles but is slit on both sides from the waist down. It provided a very soft and attractive picture.

One of the girls came over to my table and asked if I wanted a drink. I then realized that she worked there. She was slim and attractive, wearing a turquoise top with flowered embroidery. She wore no makeup, just a simple butterfly brooch in her long, silken black hair, which she had brushed to flow down the center of her back. I ordered my Coke and she brought it over. After I paid for it and started to drink, she hesitated a second and then asked if I would like to go with her. I was still quite the naïve boy from the Midwest, and only then did the penny drop. When I looked in the back and saw the other girls smiling, I finally understood that the girls were sex workers and this was their stand.

I hesitated for a few seconds, not from any moral consideration or concern about what my former primary school teacher Sister Mary Agony might think; I simply needed the time to come to grips with this unexpected rendezvous and also the realization that I had very little money on me. I decided the direct approach was the best policy, so I emptied my pockets of what I had, about fifteen dollars in military currency, and showed her. "That's all I have. Is it enough?" She frowned a bit, carefully counted the money, picked it all up, and nodded for me to follow her.

We were in what might be called a poor suburban beach

neighborhood, Vietnam style. It was several blocks of small one-story homes with metal roofs. They all had narrow fronts and extended two or three rooms back. The young girl—actually she seemed about my own age—called over a bicycle cab, or cyclo, and we sat side-by-side in front as the driver pedaled along following her directions. We rode down a back alley between two rows of houses, then she stopped him and I followed her inside.

I understood that this was her home. As we walked in the back, which was the kitchen and laundry room, I heard voices in the front room. She told me to stay there and went to join them. I heard her talking softly and then some scuffling noises as the others got up and left the house to her.

I won't go into detail about our encounter, but for me it was like a beautiful dream. I just followed her lead in all things. She gasped a little when she saw my bandages but responded as if she was a nurse, which for me she was. I guess you could say it was the final nursing of my hospital stay. She gently led me along.

Fifteen minutes later, we were back out in the alleyway where the cyclo was waiting, and it took us back to the Coke stand. I said good-bye to her and limped away to flag down a ride back to the hospital chopper pad. Now I was healed, at least in my mind, and it was time to go back to duty.

There was one final incident during my return to my unit. When I arrived at Camp Alpha at Tan Son Nhut Air Base I was in time to catch dinner at the mess hall. After that, I walked over to the wooden officers' barracks, the same one I had stayed in when I had arrived in-country more than two and a half months earlier.

As I walked through the door, I saw an officer standing by one of the double bunks at the end of the row. I could tell he had just arrived in-country because his fatigues were fresh. When he turned around I had to yell. It was one of my best buddies from officers' training and Airborne School, John W.

Leek, with the 'W' standing for Wayne, as he often let people know. I had volunteered for Vietnam, so I had arrived a couple of months early and now many of my classmates were starting to arrive in the normal rotation.

John and I sat down to talk. He had a hundred questions about the reality of functioning as a platoon leader in combat, and I tried to provide the answers. Of course, the ultimate response is that you have to experience combat yourself. One piece of advice I gave him came from a lieutenant who had served with the 1st Infantry Division and with whom I had roomed prior to shipping out to Vietnam. What he told me was, "If you think of it, do it." What he meant was that many times in the field you would be dead exhausted and setting up for the night. Possibly there would be a question of security, maybe checking out a nearby tree line for evidence of Charlie, but you might be too tired and think your men are too tired as well. Go ahead and push yourself and the men. Make sure that the tree line gets checked out. Better the guys think you are a bastard than think you are a decent guy with whom they end up dead. If you think of it, do it.

The time for lights out was soon upon us. I stripped down for bed by taking off my jungle fatigues, shirt, and trousers, to sleep in my shorts and t-shirt, as we normally did. When I had taken off my fatigues, John for the first time saw the bandages on my arm, and hip, and the big one wrapped around my right thigh. His face turned white. I hadn't realized it, but I had broken the stitches on the wound on my thigh earlier in the day and the wound had bled through the bandages. It had dried by nightfall, but it didn't look too good.

John asked me what the hell I was doing going back to my unit when I was still not healed. My answer was that when he had his own platoon he would understand. I belonged with the guys in my platoon. I could heal just as well when I was back in Cu Chi. He just shook his head.

We separated the next morning. I went to the aviation control hut to catch a chopper back to Cu Chi while John waited to find out what unit he would be assigned to. It turned out he was also assigned to the 25th Infantry Division, joining the 1st Battalion, 5th Infantry Regiment, a mechanized-infantry unit. I would see him again several times when we were both in the Cu Chi base camp. He served well and survived his time as a platoon leader and his year in Vietnam.

December 1966

The number of American military:

KIA was 385

WIA was 2,442

DOC was 85

CHAPTER 15
BACK TO THE FIELD

My return to Cu Chi was anticlimactic. Beginning the day I had been wounded, the battalion had remained on routine duty in Cu Chi as the division reserve; it not ventured out in the field except for routine security patrols around the division base camp. Nevertheless, the word was that we would be going out within a few days.

I visited the doctor who served as battalion medical officer. He cleaned my wounds and rewrapped my bandages. He shook his head when he saw the busted stitches in my thigh, and told me that, rather sewing them back up, he would let the wound heal from the inside out. He said it would leave a bigger scar, but he wanted to be careful to avoid infection. I really didn't care; he could take a look at it every couple of days. The only issue was that I had to wrap plastic around it to keep it dry when I took a shower, but that was a minor inconvenience. It was healing slowly and I was walking better every day.

My RTO had received his third Purple Heart, and thus had been rotated off the line. He deserved the break, and I would have asked that he be transferred in any case. It had been obvious in the weeks preceding the fire fight that his nerves were pretty frayed. His replacement was Bob Carnoske, a bright young guy selected by Sergeant Amado from one of the rifle squads. Bob was from St. Louis, twenty-one or so, and happy with the promotion. He showed me his favorite picture from back home, in which he was standing next to his sparkling clean '57 Chevy. I told him I thought he had his priorities right.

Bob had a visitor shortly after I got back to camp and he brought him round to meet me. It was his brother-in-law, an Air Force captain who flew the twin-engine C-130 cargo plane that was the military transport mainstay. When I asked him what missions he flew, he told me he was flying Agent Orange spraying runs over the jungle-clad area the U.S. military called the Iron Triangle. The Iron Triangle was a vast wedge of jungle along the Saigon River that included the operational boundary between the 25th Infantry Division, at Cu Chi, which is twenty miles north of Saigon, and the 1st Infantry Division, at Bien Hoa which is twenty miles east of Saigon. At the time, I thought that the aerial spraying was an odd way to wage war, but I just let it go. It wasn't until years later, when the evidence surfaced about the damage Agent Orange had done to the Vietnamese civilian population as well as American servicemen who had been exposed—including me—that I remembered the conversation.

Overall, I found the guys in the platoon pumped up. There is nothing more exhilarating then having people try to kill you and surviving. The platoon had gained a lot of respect within the battalion, and the battalion within the division. I would think about this over the years, when I read military history and accounts of the 19th century Indian wars on the western frontier of the U.S., in which this same 9th Infantry Regiment had participated. There is a warrior spirit in young men of all ethnic backgrounds that can't be denied. I can't say if it's testosterone-driven, but it is truly there. It could be this same spirit or need that drives groups of young men in slum neighborhoods to form gangs or provides the motivation for team sports. Basically, what my platoon had done was "count coup," as they said in the Old West of the warrior tactic of the American Indians. We had confronted the enemy directly and personally and come away the winner. The result was a growth in pride and confidence for everybody in the unit. I now felt that it was my job to sustain that confidence in our upcoming operations.

We soon learned that we were to leave the rubber plantations and go back to the rice paddies on the edge of the Mekong Delta. The 25th Infantry Division's area of operations (AO) was in what the military designated III Corps, which included the provinces around Saigon, west to the edge of the Mekong Delta, and north to Tay Ninh and the Cambodian border. There was no U.S. infantry division assigned to the Mekong Delta area at that time, so the 25th periodically sent a battalion to set up base alongside the Delta in Long An Province, at the western rim of its operational area. That was where Alpha Company had been when I joined it three months earlier, and that was where we were returning now.

It would be a full battalion operation, including the battery of 105mm howitzers that would support the battalion and its headquarters. To initiate the operation, the rifle companies were to carry out airmobile assaults into various zones, then sweep toward a village on a crossroads at the edge of the Delta. The other battalion units would travel by road and set up a base camp just outside the village that would be our home for the next month as we conducted operations in the area.

The airmobile assault a few days later was routine. There was no enemy fire as my company dropped off the choppers into the rice paddy or as we sorted ourselves out to start the long single-file hike along a trail through the paddies toward the village that was our objective. Captain Neilson and the company headquarters group were toward the front of the file and 2nd Platoon was bringing up the rear again.

The rainy season was well over and it was a clear, brutally

hot day. Progress was slow as the lead units checked out various farm huts along the way in search of caches of rice or weapons. We had walked more than three hours, stopping and starting, when we got word that we would be delayed for a while because the vanguard group had detained a farmer and was interrogating him. There was an ARVN soldier attached to the company headquarters group to serve as a translator and guide, and he led the questioning.

We had been waiting alongside the trail for about fifteen minutes when we heard a loud explosion from the front of the column followed by several shots in quick succession, then silence. We waited five minutes before we got word that the company commander had been wounded and a medevac chopper was on the way to fly him out. After a further fifteen minutes, the chopper arrived, picked up the captain, and took off again. Very shortly after that I got a radio call; with the captain gone I was the senior officer, and the question was what should we do? I checked the map and the trail direction and told the lead platoon to keep on moving toward the rendezvous, which looked to be only an hour's walk away.

When we entered the village, we found that the engineers had laid out a barbed-wire perimeter for the battalion just outside it, in land that was primarily rice paddy. My platoon took up its portion of the perimeter while I got the story on the captain from the company headquarters group. Apparently the ARVN interpreter had led the group in poking around a farmer's hut and found a cover over a hole in the ground. The farmer, a VC, who had hidden in the hole, was armed with his rifle, a Chinese copy of a Russian Mossin-Nagant carbine, an old World War II standby. He climbed out of the hole and handed his carbine over. Then the translator started interrogating him. For some reason, during the questioning the farmer panicked. He grabbed a hand grenade off the vest of one of the American soldiers present, pulled the pin, and dropped it in front of everyone. There was a five-second delay before the explosion, which allowed people to scramble far enough out of the way so that nobody was killed. Nonetheless, the captain was close enough to catch a lot of shrapnel. The translator, who had probably sparked the problem with his questions and interrogation methods, then pulled his .45-caliber pistol and shot the VC dead. My feeling was that it was not an inspiring episode. The interrogation had obviously turned into something of a show, with soldiers crowding around, and the captain had paid the price.

This occurred in early December and, to some extent, the episode set the tone for the next month. Although we were near a village called Binh Chanh, the campsite itself was miserable. The hard ground in the area was taken up with placement of the 105mm howitzer battery that supported the battalion. The rifle companies distributed around the perimeter were perched precariously on the rice paddy dikes. The troops built wooden huts out of the crates the 105mm artillery shells were packed in, with sandbags around the sides and ponchos spread over the top to keep out rain. But there was nothing to keep the mosquitoes out, and they ate us alive the whole month. At night, huge field rats roamed along the dikes.

When we first arrived in the camp area and I had received instructions on how to place my platoon on the perimeter, I had the troops fall into ranks so I could brief them. As I stood in front of the ranks of men, there was a tremendous explosion behind me and, without thought, in instant reaction, I found myself on the ground, facing the direction from which the noise had come.

I saw what the source of the explosion was. The 105mm gunners were firing to register their howitzers. The men knew it was coming because they were facing the guns, but I had my back to them. I got back on my feet and turned to face the ranks. I saw a lot of smiles but heard no laughter. The guys found it amusing, but they seemed they to understand that I had a right to be sensitive to loud noises. I just smiled back and got on with the briefing. This reaction to explosive sounds would stick with me for the rest of my life. Fifteen years later, while walking on a street in Washington, D.C., I found myself down on all fours and peering around after a car backfired near me. The reaction has diminished with time, but it is still there.

Many have written of combat as long periods of boredom interspersed with short periods of pure panic. This was to be a long period of boredom. Our company commander returned to us after three days. His face and arms were peppered with small shrapnel marks, but it had missed his eyes. Apart from the embarrassment of being wounded with one of our own grenades, he was okay.

Squads were dispatched on nightly ambush patrols, and on one occasion our company was sent out on a two-day sweep, but we came up with nothing.

We had a *Newsweek* correspondent fly in from Saigon, only a twenty-minute chopper ride away, to report on this new operation in the Delta because we were the first American unit to operate in that area. I am afraid he found little to report as we weren't making significant contact. I clearly remember everyone looking at him getting back on the chopper to return to Saigon and really hating the bastard for having that easy out available to him.

At one point, I felt I was doing so little that I asked the company commander if we could put together a patrol of at least fifteen soldiers, so that I could legitimately take the position of patrol leader instead of deferring to the squad leaders, whom I felt were bearing the entire burden on night patrols. My aim was just to do my job and give the squad leaders a break, but ironically it led to a bit of a squabble as they objected to their guys going out without them. I understood this but had to pull rank because I felt I needed to be seen as being involved in the field, not just sitting around supervising arrangements at the base camp.

The other issue that was surfacing was that, as good as it was to be with experienced troops when I first arrived in Vietnam more than three months earlier, many of these same troops were now counting down to the final day of their one-year overseas service. There were fewer than ninety days left until some rotated back to the States. In the language of the military, they were now "short timers." They thus had one goal in life, and that is to minimize their exposure to risk. The reasoning is that you've made it through nine months or more on the line, so don't let Charlie get you in the last two or three. Some of the troops had already started campaigning to be assigned to jobs in the division base camp, and in fact there was an unspoken policy of getting guys off the line in their last month of duty if it was at all possible. Also, I sensed a remoteness in the men when I was briefing them on the routes to be taken and points to be used on the night ambush patrols. Platoon Sergeant Amado had let me know that just maybe the patrols were stopping short and simply cooping up at an intermediate point overnight to be safe. This was dangerous, not only because they weren't providing the area coverage in the field that they were supposed to, but also because the correct location was marked on the artillery and mortar platoon fire-support maps. If fire support was required, these troops were in danger of having it fall on them in their unmarked position. I felt I had to step in and lead a patrol all the way in order to set an example.

The ambush patrol was a big nothing. We had no hint of contact, just sat on a cold, wet paddy dike on a night that was so dark I couldn't see my hand in front of my face. It was a long night of sweat and buzzing mosquitoes.

We had an ARVN unit based near us. They carried out daytime patrols, looking for situations the U.S. troops might be able to follow up on at night. I understood part of the reason for our presence was to encourage them and the rural population, so they knew that American military support was on hand.

One afternoon, at about 3:00 p.m., we were in base camp

when we heard a tremendous explosion on the other side of the village. I found out later that an ARVN patrol had been returning to camp after a day out and had tripped what is now called an improvised explosive device, an IED. Two men were killed and several were wounded. The ARVNs had made a mistake by taking the same trail back from their patrol that they had taken on the way out.

The main thought that I was left with was that someone in the village must have seen the VC setting up that booby trap and said nothing. Possibly, it was the villagers themselves who had set the explosives in place. That spoke volumes about how welcome government and American. troops were in that district.

Years later I was to learn that this area, Long An Province, had been contested between the government forces and the Viet Minh when they fought against the French. The Viet Minh had been fighting here for more than twenty years, and according to at least one analyst's subsequent report, the war had already been lost in terms of popular support of the same population years before the U.S. military arrived. The fact that both we and the government troops had to live behind wire, with nowhere we could go unarmed, attested to that reality.

During the month we were out there, I had severe health problems. Somehow I had drunk or eaten something that gave me terrible diarrhea. The battalion doc gave me medicines, but nothing worked and I spent ten or twelve days completely miserable, struggling to stay on top of issues with the platoon. In that sense, it was good that the company was primarily sending out squad patrols. When you go through combat leadership training courses, you are in excellent health and great physical condition. What you learn only in the field is that many times you have to exercise that leadership when you are largely incapacitated for one reason or another. The expectations are nonetheless the same. Years later, I read about an American army group called

Merrill's Marauders, which fought in northern Burma during World War II. Almost to a man, the Marauders suffered from diarrhea so bad that they just cut holes in the seat of their pants to ensure they wouldn't foul themselves. It made my couple of weeks of misery look like nothing, but at the time I was just struggling to cope with my own reality and still do my job.

The other thing that was bothering me—much more serious, it turned out—was my right ear. I had suffered from constant aching and ringing in my ear since the explosion in the rubber plantation. When I had first gotten back to Cu Chi, I went to the company medic, Spec. 4 Maxwell, and asked him what he thought might help. He said it was probably just an infection and gave me some liquid to put in my ear to clean it up. I administered the dose in front of him and yelped like crazy at the intense pain. I felt as if it nearly took my head off. Later, we got the battalion surgeon to take a look at the ear. He said it wasn't infected, but I did have a hole or perforation in my eardrum from the explosion. He said I was okay for duty and that it would probably heal itself over time. My battalion spent Christmas and New Year in that miserable rice paddy camp and the pain did not go away.

My concern was my hearing. Being out on night patrol, especially on absolutely black nights, good hearing was your greatest asset. You had to hear Charlie before he heard you. We had night-vision devices at the time, but they weren't used on routine patrols for fear of their falling into enemy hands.

We got word that the Bob Hope USO show was coming to Vietnam on a Christmas tour, but the entertainers got nowhere near our unit down in the Delta. We were told that the troupe would entertain in Bien Hoa, north of Saigon, where the 1st Infantry Division was based. It didn't do a thing for us as a unit, though a few guys were given passes to go up and catch the show.

We celebrated a dreary Christmas and New Year with patrols going out, but there was no contact.

I went back to see the doc about my ear early in the first week of January. In the meantime, he had apparently consulted with some other doctors and had changed his opinion. Now he was afraid that, if I persisted in the field, the open eardrum would become infected and I would permanently lose my hearing in that ear. I asked what could be done and he told me I needed surgery to close the hole.

I agonized about leaving the troops again, but then reasoned that a short stay in the hospital would heal the ear and help me get over my acute diarrhea. I figured that would be back in a short time. Unfortunately, it would turn out I was very wrong.

January 1967

The number of American military:

KIA was 403

WIA was 3,456

DOC was 112

CHAPTER 16
CAMP ZAMA

At the end of the first week of January, I left my platoon for the second time to go back to Cu Chi to pick up orders for the hospital. There I learned that this would not be as simple a trip as before. This operation had to be done in Japan, at the Camp Zama army hospital outside of Tokyo. I spent one night at the army hospital in Saigon and the next day I was loaded onto a cargo jet at Ton Son Nhut bound for Yokota Air Force Base. The plane was loaded with guys on stretchers, plus a handful like me who were mobile but had some condition that needed treatment that couldn't be rendered in Vietnam. I was really confused. I knew I was doing the right thing for my health—like most young guys, I found the thought of any disability impossible to accept—but it really felt like I was going in the wrong direction as far as my duty was concerned.

We landed seven hours later. It was nighttime in Japan. The experience was in stark contrast to my introduction to Vietnam four months earlier. As we descended the rear ramp of the plane, the impact of the below-freezing air was a shock, especially as I was dressed in my jungle fatigues. Light snow was falling and the buildings and offices on the base were still decorated with Christmas lights. The transition was just too much. I felt tears in my eyes and slowed my pace into the reception area so that I could regain control of myself.

It is difficult even today to describe the emotional swings I went through during that period in Japan. The army hospital at Camp Zama seemed like paradise to a soldier coming straight from the field. It was clean, had great food (of course, any food was better than the meals in the field), and on balance you might have thought you were back in the States.

Camp Zama was a fairly large administrative base. The hospital and the quarters for its staff were a fifteen-minute taxi ride away. That made a big difference to the atmosphere at the hospital, because the doctors and nurses on the staff wore civilian clothes when they were off duty. There was a small officers' club adjacent to the hospital, and all the staff were very relaxed regarding military protocol. It seemed more like a civilian setting then a military one. I was unaware of this right away as I was being processed for surgery on my right eardrum.

I met with the doctor who would do the procedure after a couple of days, and he scheduled the operation a similar interval later. As I understood it, they were going to reopen the healed edges of the eardrum and leave a hole in it. They would then insert a covering that would replace the eardrum, and allow the wounds to heal again. The covering would melt away, leaving me with a whole eardrum once more, but one that would inevitably be scarred. The doctor assured me that my hearing would be good, but there might be some diminution at the higher register of sound. That was okay to me.

What came next was a bit of a shock and did *not* sound okay. I had assumed this process would be similar to my hospitalization in Vung Tau a couple of months earlier: come in, get treated, and a week or so later be back on my way to the troops. Now the doctor told me it, would take a month or more for the eardrum to heal. He put a positive spin on it, pointing out that this was a good opportunity for me to take a break. He told me to spend a little time being a tourist in Japan, "Just don't fall on your head."

I agonized over it, but there was essentially nothing I could do. I was in the grip of the system. Getting back to the troops wasn't the simple matter it had been when I left Vung Tau. I couldn't just walk out to a chopper pad and hitch a ride. So I let go and decided to allow things to come as they would.

A couple of weeks after the operation, thanks to some kind hospital staff, I was included in a small group that visited a Japanese skiing and hot springs resort, Kusatsu, located a few hours' drive away from Camp Zama in the Japanese Alps northwest of Tokyo. We left early on a Friday morning and arrived about midday, in time to get in some skiing. This was a first for me, but I was able to catch on fairly quickly and had some fun without breaking anything.

After skiing, I was introduced to a unique Japanese custom, the ofuro or communal hot bath. The hotel had two of these—one for men and one for women—rather than the traditional baths of the Japanese past, which served both sexes at once. I went through the ritual washing and scrubbing first and then sat in what was more a steaming swimming pool than a bath. Immediately alongside where I sat in the steaming water, there was a plate glass window looking down the mountainside to a forest and a small village several hundred feet below. There was a light snow falling and smoke was spiraling up from some of the chimneys in the village. The beauty and serenity was such that if I had been a tourist, fresh from the States, it would still have made a tremendous impression on me. But being just weeks away from the stink, sweat, and fear of the jungle in Vietnam, it was utter magic. The boy from Milwaukee had no idea such beauty and tranquility existed in the world. I had found that outside of Tokyo, Japan was a fantastically beautiful country. I made up my mind that when I was finished in the military I would find a way to return and learn more of it.

I might have left the war for a few moments, but the war didn't leave me. On returning to Camp Zama at the end of January, I received a letter from Platoon Sergeant Amado. He had bad news. A week or so after I left the platoon, it had returned to Cu Chi for a few days and then mounted an airmobile assault into a new area in which the division had intelligence that the VC were very active. The company entered a hot LZ, over which the chopper was taking fire before it even set down. Sergeant Bobby Wood, the young squad leader who had warned me against sitting on the end seat in the chopper, had done so himself and taken a round in his side as it was touching down. He never even got off the chopper but fell onto the floor as the other troopers jumped off. The crew chief tried to help him as the chopper lifted off and headed straight for the nearest hospital, which was in Saigon, less than twenty minutes away. When they touched down on the roof of the hospital Sergeant Wood was dead from shock and loss of blood.

Sergeant Wood was one of the most popular guys in the platoon, young and handsome, well over six feet tall and always positive, always going to the front when we were in the field. The news devastated me, just as Sergeant Amado said it had devastated the platoon. I have never forgotten and will never forget Sergeant Bobby Wood. His is one of the names I touch whenever I visit the Vietnam Memorial in Washington, D.C. I also found his name on the Vietnam Memorial in Albany, New York, when I visited there.

Sergeant Amado continued, saying that if there was any way I could avoid coming back, I should. "This war is no good" he wrote. I understood him being burned out and upset. He and Sergeant Wood were with the original group from the 25th Division that had arrived in Vietnam from Hawaii the previous March and April. He was nearing the end of his tour. I wrote back to him to try to be as positive as I could, but there was little to be positive about.

I was also learning that the medical staff of the Camp Zama hospital, mostly the doctors, were not enthusiastic about the war in Vietnam either. Nothing too overt was said, but there was an apparent lack of eagerness to turn their patients out just to ship them back to Vietnam to get wounded again, or killed. This was different from the hospital staff I had encountered in Vietnam. There, they had more incoming casualties than they could handle at times, and the feeling in Vietnam generally seemed to be that the sooner they could get you out of that bed and on your way back to duty the better.

While I was in the hospital, there continued to be a steady stream of new patients from Vietnam. Just as many of my friends from officers' training had followed me to the war after a month or two, now some of those friends followed me on the path to the hospital in Japan. A good friend, John Hertzler, from Pennsylvania, who had served as a rifle platoon leader with the 4th Infantry Division in the central highlands of Vietnam, came through in need of surgery on a serious leg wound. John was a unique case in several ways. He was very muscular and had been a college wrestler. Though not of an Amish family himself, he had been raised in an Amish area in Pennsylvania and had adopted some of their religious beliefs. Before we left OCS, we talked about the probability of going to Vietnam and leading a rifle platoon. He told me he didn't think he could kill another human being. When I asked what he intended to do, he told me that he would lead but not shoot. I was more than a little astonished and didn't know what to say, but I felt absolute respect for the strength of his religious beliefs. He was not the only officer I met who would carry a weapon but let people know he wasn't going to fire it, but that's a story for later.

John brought news of several of our classmates serving as rifle platoon leaders who had been killed in action, one, Al Guyer, served with C Company of the 2nd Battalion, 173rd Airborne Brigade. Al was a Golden Gloves boxing champion from Kansas City. He had been killed in an operation near the Cambodian border following the only mass parachute assault in Vietnam.

As I wrote before, the last time I saw Al was when he was arriving at the Jungle Expert School as I was leaving. He had wished me good luck, and then he was gone. I hadn't said good luck to him. I believed Al was the kind of guy that didn't need luck. I believed he could overcome anything.

Other casualties were Jim Hill, a slim, athletic man with an engaging smile who also served with the 173rd and died in the jungles near Cambodia. And Sam James, who was killed on an operation with the 1st Infantry Division. Again, it always seemed as if it was the guys who you remembered as real leaders who were the ones going down. It was a steady stream of depressing news, but it was soon to be followed, near the end of my hospital stay, by the most crushing blow of all.

I encountered some new casualties who had been serving with the 25th, and they brought word of a major fight my company had been involved in. This was in the days when there wasn't any form of written information available to the troops except newspapers and letters. We had Armed Forces Radio in Japan, but it didn't cover any detail of the war in Vietnam. Word of events involving specific units in action travelled slowly.

Thus it was more than a week after it occurred, the first week of March, before I learned that my Alpha Company had been in combat with and was overrun by a Viet Cong battalion in the early morning hours of February 26. Ironically, it wasn't too far from the location at which my platoon had attacked the VC camp several months earlier. First and 2nd platoons (2nd being mine) of Alpha Company were providing security for an engineer battalion that was tasked with clearing the forest and developing a road leading from the Cu Chi base camp toward the Saigon River. The task would take several weeks, so VC had plenty of time to study what was going on, gather their forces, and prepare a plan of attack.

February 1967

The number of American military:

KIA was 403

WIA was 3,853

DOC was 88

CHAPTER 17
NOT PRESENT FOR DUTY

The language of the military report is dry and limited. "Operational Report—Lessons Learned," written by the 25th Infantry Division in October 1967 and covering the February 1 through April 30 1967 quarter, describes the action as follows:

> "Operation Ala Moana was conducted in Hau Nghia province to destroy VC forces, supplies and base camps near the Division base camp at Cu Chi, and in the Filhol plantation. In February an additional mission was undertaken to clear the road from Cu Chi to Phu Hoa Dong (map coordinates XT 709 195) and clear the surrounding wooded area.
>
> On 22 February the 1st Brigade dispatched Alpha Company, 4th Battalion 9th Infantry Regiment to the Filhol plantation (XT 701 190) to clear the road from Cu Chi to Phu Hoa Dong, and to provide security for attached Engineer elements in clearing the wooded area. At 26 February at 0030 Company A was attacked by an estimated Viet Cong (VC) battalion (probably 1st Battalion Military Region IV) using mortars, rifle grenades and human wave assault tactics. The attack was repelled by AW (automatic

> weapons) artillery, gunships and air strikes. The Division base reaction force (Troop A, 3rd Squadron, 4th Cavalry, and Company B, 4th Battalion, 9th Infantry Regiment) was committed at 0310 on 26 February and linked up with Company A at 0410 on 26 February. Action terminated at 0800 hours. There was no further contact in February."

The report later stated VC killed in action as 113 by body count with another 33 VC estimated KIA whose bodies had been removed by the VC. Captured were two U.S. made Browning Automatic Rifles (BARs), one AK-47 rifle, one Chicom carbine with grenade launcher, one Russian light machine gun, two RPG-2 rocket launchers with 18 RPG-2 rounds, one M1 rifle, and one .50 caliber machine gun tripod. A prisoner of war, Huynh Van Huynh, was captured in the area and identified as an assistant squad leader from the 2nd Platoon, 5th Company, 1st Battalion, Military Region IV.

In later pages the report noted that with regard to "item (c) Ice Cream, an issue was made every other day to troops at Cu Chi base with 1,477 gallons per week coming from Saigon and 903 gallons a week manufactured in Cu Chi."

After ice cream, in the section described as a review of division strength, the report cited 116 officers and men killed in action during the period and 1,239 wounded in action.

That is about as dry as you can get, but, of course, a modern army must track *all* the numbers, ice cream as well as KIA. But for me, there was one important number missing.

One particular soldier was not present for duty on February 26, 1967. Twenty-six members of my company were killed in action and another forty were wounded, but *I* was not there to help. *I* was absent from duty, still in the hospital in Japan. That failure to be on hand when I was needed has haunted me all my life. Some wounds never heal.

The way I learned of the fight was through the hospital

grapevine. Someone who knew that I was assigned to the 25th Infantry Division approached me to let me know that a new batch of wounded had come in from Vietnam. A number of 25th Infantry Division soldiers were included. I didn't know any of them personally, but when I went to talk with them they told me it was Alpha Company that had taken the majority of the casualties. For me, the news was a ticket to Hell. I was sick, shocked, and fell into the blackest depression. I had let the troops down. I should have been there. I should have died with them. Nothing else was acceptable.

The Associated Press, in a news report a week later, provided a more intimate human face to the killing of that night. The title of the article was "Questions Linger About Battle Horror." Beyond the shock of the fighting itself, it went into the issue of how some ARVN troops attached to Alpha Company had handled themselves in the fighting. Some troopers told of an ARVN interpreter shooting an American soldier, Staff Sergeant Ray Nixon, before being killed by another American. This issue was made more confusing by the fact that ARVN uniforms were found in the backpacks of the VC KIA and it was understood they had orders to change into those uniforms once they had penetrated the perimeter. Another Alpha Company soldier told of an ARVN soldier, sharing the same bunker, who was too scared to fire at the attackers or to leave the bunker when it was overrun. He was later found dead.

I counted seven men from my platoon who had been killed. There were many names I didn't recognize because soldiers I had known, including Sergeant Amado, had rotated out of Vietnam in the weeks of my absence and had been replaced.

It was too late to be any use, but I went to the doctors and persuaded them to agree that I could return immediately to Vietnam and my unit.

***

The plane ride back to Saigon was in total contrast to my initial flight six months earlier. There was no chatter at all. Everyone on the flight had been wounded in combat and knew what they were returning to. We all settled into our own wells of silence, wrapped in blankets to combat the plane's overactive air conditioning.

It was a long, cold, dark flight. The beast of war was waiting, and we all understood that it was complete chance as to whether we would survive or not. My thinking was very clear. I needed to get back on the line and carry out what I had been trained to do and was confident I could do. I didn't have a death wish, but I was ready to accept whatever might come in order to redeem myself.

When I reported in to Alpha Company in Cu Chi I received a very unwelcome shock. I went directly to the new company commander, told him I was reporting in, and wanted to return to combat duty. He replied that I no longer had a platoon. A new officer had been assigned to lead 2nd Platoon, and, in any case, virtually all the men I had served with had been killed or wounded, and were now off the line or had been transferred back to the States. When I told him I really wanted to get back on the line, he suggested I try Charlie Company, which he knew was short one platoon leader.

The commander of Charlie Company said he would be glad to take me, but the battalion commander had to approve. The next morning, I reported to the battalion commander, who was happy to see me but told me I couldn't revert to being a platoon leader. He had other plans for me. He considered me to have potential as a career officer and wanted me to work as an assistant staff officer in the battalion S3 shop.

The 3 shop was the plans and training component of the battalion headquarters, and the officer designated S3 was a major. His were the people who had put together the patrol plan for the night I was wounded several months earlier. I would be reporting to a captain who was the assistant S3, and helping to draw up and monitor the battle actions of the battalion's companies and platoons. This was considered a plum assignment for an officer of any rank and an important place to get one's ticket punched for career officers.

I protested the best I could but to no avail. The battalion CO liked me and was pleased I had pushed to get a platoon. He said he admired my spirit, but he had still said no. From his point of view, I had my combat ticket punched already, having been awarded a Purple Heart and a medal for valor, the Silver Star, following the patrol in the Filhol rubber plantation. I had received this medal while I was in the hospital in Japan, once the paperwork caught up with me.

The CO pushed me to apply for a Regular Army commission rather than the Reserve commission that I held in common with most junior officers. He said he would give my application a strong recommendation. He urged me to consider a career in the army. I told him I would think about it.

I can't blame the battalion CO; he was just trying to reward me for what he saw as good service, and he wanted to help push me up the career ladder as hard as he could. This was the same officer who had arranged the phony field exercise for Lieutenant B. His reality, like the reality of virtually all of the military's top officers, wasn't the Vietnam War, it was the war for promotion. By achieving leadership of an infantry battalion in combat, he had taken a major step towards being promoted to a general's rank someday. Combat was just one part of the path, though; he would need to attend Command and General Staff College and finish near the top of the class, plus some staff hoops to jump through after that.

Years after the war in Vietnam was over, I had the opportunity to meet and become a friend of David Hackworth, known as Hack by those close to him. Hack was an infantry officer who became a legend during the war. When Vietnam first heated up in 1964, Hack, then a major who had won many awards for valor during two tours in the Korean War, had volunteered to go over. At the time, the officers in the Military Personnel Center, MILPERCEN, the human resource gods of assignments, had refused him on the grounds that he had "too much combat experience." The career management message was that Vietnam service was good for promotion, but that it shouldn't pre-empt the other tickets that needed to be punched. Hack had turned down an assignment to the Command & General Staff College and would do so again in his effort to get to Vietnam. He achieved his aim the following year, 1965, with the 101st Airborne Division, and he ended up leading the 1st Battalion, 327th Infantry Regiment, with distinction.

While I was serving at Fort Benning in 1965, I had heard mid-level officers who hadn't served in the Korean War and had not had an opportunity to get their combat tickets punched, joking that Vietnam "wasn't much of a war, but it's the only war we got."

This sort of thinking of war as a means of promotion permeated the consciousness of career officers and thus affected the leadership outlook of the entire Vietnam operation. The parachute assault by the 173rd Airborne Brigade in February 1967 was a good example.

There was no need for a combat parachute jump other than the necessity for airborne generals and field-grade officers to get a gold combat jump star placed on the jump wings they wore on their chests. There were not enough planes available for the entire brigade to jump. I imagine there must have been a really epic pushing-and-shoving battle amongst the senior staff officers to see who would get one of the limited slots aboard a C-130. A helicopter assault would have served as well, and probably better. In any case, Special Forces detachments penetrated the area first to ensure the troops weren't jumping into a hot LZ. This PR opportunity for the airborne army couldn't be allowed to go wrong. The 173rd was a first-class outfit, it did run into enemy forces several days afterwards, and it sustained causalities, including classmates of mine, but the jump itself wasn't necessary.

For me, it wasn't about career. Prior to Vietnam, I had truly loved most of my service in the army, jumping out of airplanes, running through the woods. All of the boys' world stuff was great fun, but I wasn't sure I wanted a career. What I wanted, what I needed now, was redemption. I had failed my men by sitting on my ass in Japan when they were fighting for their lives, and I desperately desired to get back on line and kill Charlie. Anything else felt like a cop-out to me.

In the end, I had no choice but to do as the battalion commander ordered. I was going to be a staff officer. I was crushed. My vision of redeeming myself through action in the field was gone. I had no choice but to accept, though much later I would find another possibility open to me.

March 1967

The number of American military:

KIA was 421

WIA was 6,314

DOC was 142

CHAPTER 18
A DIFFERENT VIEW OF THE WAR

Working in the battalion S3 shop meant no more night patrols and no more aerial assaults, but it was not necessarily an end to going out to the field. It had apparently become dogma in the 25th Infantry Division that the battalions belonged out in the bush somewhere, but definitely not in the Cu Chi base camp. In fact, I wasn't to spend more than a few nights in the camp for the rest of my tour. That was fine with me as at least it held out the possibility of participating in some action that would help me to atone for my absence.

A week or so after rejoining the battalion in mid-March, we flew down again to the edge of the Delta, to an area that was nicknamed the Pineapple Patch. I presume there were pineapples there, but I never saw one. The terrain was mixed brushy scrub forest and some rice paddies.

The rifle companies had made the usual airmobile assaults in the area surrounding the site for the battalion headquarters. The headquarters staff, which now included me, flew in a couple of hours later on a Chinook helicopter, which also carried equipment for the battalion tactical operations center (TOC). We were to set up in an area secured by one of the infantry companies.

While we were still several hundred feet up, the Chinook took small arms fire. We could hear the rounds pinging off the walls of the chopper. When we hit the ground and unloaded, there was no incoming fire, so I assumed we were below the tree line and out of sight of the VC. I asked one of the crewmen and he said it was nothing, just rifle fire. He said that when they were receiving .51-caliber machine gun fire it was a completely different sound, like somebody banging on the fuselage with a sledgehammer. He said *that* noise would get his attention.

I'm sure it sounds stupid to say it now, but I felt a little better; at least I was getting shot at. It held out promise that I might be able to do something worthwhile in terms of getting back at Charlie.

That feeling didn't last long. During the afternoon and into the early evening, I was busy helping to set up the TOC, which was being sandbagged by troops, and establishing radio communication with the outlying companies.

In the early evening, I was relieved on the TOC radio. As I went outside, I understood that we were taking sporadic small arms fire from around the perimeter and that a couple of the rifle company guys had been hit. This shouldn't have been my concern. As a smart staff officer, I should have gone back into the well-sandbagged TOC and sat in a corner until things quieted down, or at least lay down outside in a nearby hole in the ground behind a couple of sandbags. I didn't do either of those things.

I wanted to be involved in the shootout, however limited my contribution might be. I took my M-16, put on my steel pot and web gear, and moved through the dark toward the rifle company's perimeter positions where the fire was coming in. I could barely see, but I was able to talk with a soldier who pointed out to me roughly where the fire was coming from. As I prepared to move forward, he told me to watch out for a medic who was working on a guy who had been shot in the leg and was lying on the ground just in front of us. I told him okay, but then, after a few paces, I almost stepped on something on the ground. It was the wounded guy's leg! At least it was his good leg, not the one he had been shot in.

The medic told me to move out of the way, so I did. I knelt down, looking to see what fire might be coming in and where I could help out. But that was it. The incoming fire had stopped. Charlie was through for the night. I waited about twenty minutes, careful to stay out of the way, and then made my slow trek back to the hole in the ground outside the TOC to lie down for the night.

I really felt like a fool. The incident showed me that, as a staff officer, I was a fifth wheel for the rifle companies. They didn't need me blundering around their perimeters, attempting to redeem myself in some way. It hit me that I was probably the only guy in the perimeter who wanted Charlie to come at us. I stewed over it a while, but then I understood that I had better accept the limitations of my new role and do the best I could with it.

We spent about ten more days in the Pineapple Patch, where I slowly became accustomed to the work of the S3 shop. During that period, I received another piece of bad news. An officer I knew and respected greatly from OCS, Lieutenant Rupert Sargent, had recently been assigned to Bravo Company. He had been in officers' training in the class prior to mine, but I knew of him by reputation as he was number-one in his class and he was very athletic in appearance. I remember telling the officers I served with what a great addition he would be to the battalion. I meant to find time to look him up and welcome him. Then, within days, I learned that he had been killed on a patrol outside the Cu Chi base camp perimeter. There had been sniper fire and reports of sniper hiding holes in the ground outside the base camp area. Troops under the leadership of Lieutenant Sargent were sent out to sweep the area outside the wire where the sniper fire had been coming from. They found an entrance to a hiding hole that was booby trapped with an explosive charge. They threw grenades in an unsuccessful effort to set off the charge, and then a VC popped up and they shot him. They went forward to check further, but another VC appeared and threw two hand grenades at Lieutenant Sargent and the lead group. Lieutenant Sargent was close enough that he was able to turn and throw his body on top of the grenades. The grenades went off, killing Lieutenant Sargent. The others in his group were only lightly wounded because of his sacrifice.

I grieved for him. Rupert Sargent was among the best of the soldiers we had to offer, and it increasingly seemed to be that it was the best who were being killed. After I left Vietnam, I learned that the army had awarded him the Medal of Honor for his heroism that day. His family, however, were Jehovah's Witnesses and very much against all war, so they refused to accept the medal. Lieutenant Sargent had a wife and children. Some years later, I made a point of writing to his family in Hampton Roads, Virginia, to let them know what a fine officer and soldier I thought he was.

I was a minor player in the S3 shop. The movements of the line companies in the field were planned and coordinated by the battalion S3. The battalion CO would be on the radio, but the S3 was always at his right hand, advising. The captain I reported to handled the TOC during the day, when the companies were on the move. I took over the radio at night and monitored the various ambush patrols that the companies sent out. There was contact every day, but it was limited to shoot-outs with a few VC here and there, or finding an occasional rice or small arms cache. Nothing really big.

One thing that occurred at this time involved another target on the careerist list of special items to go for. This was the possibility of an Air Medal. The battalion had an H-23 observation chopper assigned to it that we could call on as required and as the action justified. This was in addition to a Huey UH-1D slick ship that the battalion CO could use for command and control; he flew over troops in the field and told them how to maneuver. One of the things the troops on the ground hated most was struggling through rice paddies in mud up to their knees in 100-degree heat with a lieutenant colonel flying around in circles a couple of hundred feet above, telling them to move faster because Charlie was getting away. “Really, sir? Why don’t you come down here and move faster with us?”

As a platoon leader, I had used the H-23 several times for daylight aerial recons of ground I would be leading an ambush patrol over during the night. Our model had three seats; the pilot sat in the middle and the passenger or passengers sat on either side of him. The pilot and passengers were encased in a Plexiglas bubble that included the doors, but in combat we took the doors off to ensure we could get in and out as quickly as possible, as well as to save weight.

The captain I now reported to was a career officer who served as assistant S3. One of the first things he brought up was the issue of who was going to be credited with the flying time for aerial reconnaissance in the H-23. I was completely unaware of this opportunity, so he took a few minutes to clue me in, emphasizing that he had first call on flight time to ensure he qualified for an Air Medal. He presumed I would also want flight time for the same reason.

Let me explain what this captain was about. The military has a medal that may be awarded to aviators or aviation support personnel who exhibit unusual bravery in action, at risk to their lives. That medal is the Distinguished Flying Cross. At some point in World War II, the Army Air Forces establishment decided they wanted to have a flight-related medal that could be awarded to all flight-crew members serving in combat areas for meritorious service. That medal was the Air Medal. Now this medal is several steps down the rank ladder, number eleven in precedence, but it was still a “gong,” as British military slang would have it. It was another ribbon to add to the row above the left breast pocket on your military uniform, and would be listed in your service record. Thus, career officers, who were always on the lookout for any item to give them an edge at review time, highly valued adding this gong to their collection. To qualify for the medal, one had to be a current crewmember (or a non-crewmember on flying status), where aerial flight was a consistent part of duties over a long period of time, six months or more.

The American military is devoted to gongs. When you look at senior officers and spot five or six lines of ribbons pinned above the left breast pocket, you can be sure the bottom four or five rows are not medals for valor, but just "been there, done that" awards. For instance, there was a medal given for just being in Vietnam for an extended period during the war, the Vietnam Service Medal, and another medal for simply being in the military during that period, the National Defense Medal. In addition, the Vietnamese government awarded one of their medals to all foreign military who served in Vietnam. These been-there medals begin to add up and, while I understand the good intentions in recognizing a soldier's service in distant and difficult parts of the world, over the years it has occurred to me that our top military officers sometimes look as if they are characters in a Gilbert and Sullivan comic opera with rows of been-there ribbons running out of sight underneath their uniform lapel. Certainly the emergence of the victorious North Vietnamese top military leaders in uniforms of unadorned simplicity at the end of the war offered a startling counterpoint to our leadership's fascination with decorations of all kinds.

The captain's point was that by consistently calling on the H-23 to ferry him on observation flights for planning operations, he could claim such non-crew, duty-obligated flight status and create the circumstances which would allow the battalion commander to write him up for an Air Medal on completion of his tour. By the same token, the battalion commander and the major who served as S3 would also qualify, because of their frequent flights in the Huey command-and-control chopper, overseeing the troop movements on the ground.

Coming into my new position, I had no idea about all this bureaucratic sleight of hand, and I shocked the captain when I told him I had no qualms about yielding all the air time to him, except for when he thought I should be utilizing it as part of my job. I had no interest in maneuvering to gain medals, though, frankly, my lack of interest showed my ignorance once again of the competitive requirements of career officer evaluation wars. But I can't really blame any of these officers for wanting to work the system to get the most advantageous career positioning. Officer evaluation wars are fierce and unforgiving. As time went on, however, I continued to learn how this career-first motivation frequently skewed an officer's views of what was necessary, often at the expense of getting the job in Vietnam done properly.

April 1967

The number of American military:

KIA was 436

WIA was 4,964

DOC was 116

CHAPTER 19
THE LAST MOVE

We left the Pineapple Patch and moved back to Cu Chi at the beginning of April, with less than a week to get organized before our next battalion movement. I didn't know it at the time, but this was to be the last move I made with the battalion.

The riverine-trained and -equipped 9th Infantry Division, newly arrived in Vietnam from its organization point in Colorado and jungle training in Hawaii, was moving into the Mekong Delta area. Thus, the 25th Infantry Division would now focus primarily toward the east, in the area known as the Iron Triangle which lays along the Saigon River and northward toward Tay Ninh and the Cambodian border.

As part of this refocusing, my Manchu Regiment was going north to a forested area about two-thirds of the way to Tay Ninh, near the town of Trang Bang. The specific area was called the Ho Bo Woods, and it was located more than twelve miles north of Cu Chi, closer to the terminus of the Ho Chi Minh Trail, just across the Cambodian border. We were to set up a camp for the battalion headquarters, and the rifle companies would operate deeper into the forest in an effort to interdict VC supply routes. This area had seen active fighting the previous year by other regiments in the division. In particular Alpha Company, 1/27, had been hit hard after an airmobile assault in

July and had been forced to withdraw by helicopter after sustaining twenty-five killed and thirty-two wounded. They left sixteen American KIA behind on the field. The general feeling in the battalion was that this was Indian country and that we would be seeing action for sure.

This was a unique move in that we transported the entire battalion headquarters and support groups by truck in a major convoy. It was a new direction for us, north along the main highway toward Trang Bang and the not-too-distant Cambodian border. As the convoy proceeded, the rifle companies made aerial assaults into various areas of a section of the Ho Bo Woods. Our goal was to link up at the end of the day with one of the rifle companies and set up a perimeter in the woods.

I was still of the mind that I wanted Charlie to come after us so I could play some active combat role. I was thus happy to be on the move and happy at the prospect of entering an area that was supposedly important to Charlie.

We started up the main road, which had some asphalt sections, heading north. There were no real villages, just clusters of homes along the road here and there. Then we branched off onto an increasingly narrow dirt road that led into the forest. I didn't expect any incidents along the way, and there weren't any. The VC never seemed to react to any initial move we made; they stayed back to study what the move might mean, to learn if it would be repeated on a regular basis, and to divine an advantageous time to attack. The VC were in no rush. They had been fighting their war for more than twenty years already and their patience was a perfect counterpoint to the impatience of the U.S. military.

We left the trucks in mid-afternoon and moved several kilometers by foot, further into the woods to an area where the great Minnesota woodsman, Paul Bunyan, had apparently been let loose to swing his ax. There were large craters everywhere and entire uprooted trees lay in a sideways forest that was almost impossible to traverse, even on foot. This had been the target of a B-52 bomb strike at some time within the previous month or so. There must have been some intelligence of a large VC or NVA unit moving through the area and, in the absence of infantry units to engage them directly, division headquarters had called for an Arc Light mission, which was the code name given to a B-52 tactical strike.

For the most part, we were happy to use the site of the bombing as a night position. The craters provided ready-made foxholes for many of us. Those who weren't in the craters could dig in, as I did, in what was called a two-by-two-by-you, a hole two feet deep, two feet wide, and long enough to fit our height, with piles of dirt in an embankment to catch bullets or shrapnel. When we were on the move and not in contact, this type of hole was considered adequate.

As night fell, the rifle company sent out two squad-size ambush patrols that hiked a kilometer out in different directions. Two listening posts with, two soldiers each, were also put out just a hundred meters from the perimeter. The ground was dry, the rainy season had not really started yet, and I was ready for a quiet night. I didn't expect Charlie to react to our presence so quickly.

It started about 10:00 p.m. with a sharp whistling sound I had never heard before, and then a tremendous explosion that caused the earth to shake beneath me. I had been asleep off and on, thinking it was going to be a long night, not really comfortable in my hole in the ground.

The first explosion was followed by another, and then another.

I was sorry as hell that I hadn't dug deeper. I hugged the bottom of my foxhole as closely as I could, grabbing at the dirt, trying to throw more of it out and getting lower any way possible. Shells kept whistling in and exploding all around us. These weren't mortar shells. Mortar shells only made a soft coughing noise when they were fired and were virtually silent as they came in.

These explosions were much stronger. They were high-velocity artillery shells, and the noise, the impact, and the fear they generated were tremendous. I couldn't think of anything except digging deeper, clawing, and praying for survival.

Then it stopped. The shelling hadn't lasted long in real time, only fifteen minutes or so, maybe a bit less, but for those of us on the ground it was the longest fifteen minutes of our lives. What the hell was it? I could hear that question asked repeatedly, along with cursing, yelling, and cries for a medic throughout the camp.

I didn't move for a while; I just lay there. I wasn't a medic and we weren't under direct attack, so there was nothing for me to do. After a few minutes, I sat up to try and hear better what was going on with the battalion command group, which was in a crater only twenty meters from me. I wondered what orders might be given. I heard the battalion CO on the radio, reporting back to Brigade. He was reporting that we had been shelled, and he demanded to know what the hell was going on.

We had had no reports of NVA artillery in the area, but this had definitely been artillery fire. This was not as common in our part of South Vietnam as it was in the northern areas of I Corps and II Corps, where NVA units were operating. We had not been on the receiving end of artillery fire before, and the whole unit was in shock.

I heard the report being made on the radio that we had two dead and several wounded. Evacuation of the wounded would have to wait until morning as there was no easily available space big enough for a medevac chopper at night. A cleared area for the chopper to land would have to be blasted among the trees in the morning.

The rest of the night was quiet. In the morning, I went over to the battalion command group and got a report. The artillery fire came from an ARVN 105mm artillery unit. They said they had not been informed that a U.S. Army unit was moving into the area. They were firing a routine pattern of harassment-and-interdiction fire—H&I fire—as part of their plan to stop Charlie from moving through the area. This type of fire did not focus on observed targets: someone just picked an area, usually at night, where intelligence stated that Charlie *might* be moving troops or supplies. It was a common and pretty much useless tactic in Vietnam. What it normally meant was that one gun would be fired every ten seconds or so, rather than the whole battery of six 105mm howitzers at one time. This was a lifesaver for us. If all six 105s had been fired at the same time over a sustained period in what the artillery called "fire for effect," the area would have been devastated and our casualties would have been at least ten times the number we in fact sustained. But that was small comfort to those of us on the ground.

Everyone in the unit was dumbfounded. Either our command had not clearly communicated our movement to our ARVN ally, resulting in our soldiers being killed or, as an increasingly popular theory had it, the ARVN unit was really on Charlie's side and had used this opportunity to feign misunderstanding of the situation in order to shell an American unit. The result of either belief was that our leadership was considered pretty stupid and morale instantly sank very low.

Stories of the soldiers who had been killed circulated rapidly. One soldier was the RTO for the commanding officer of the infantry company securing the site at which we had camped for the night. During the shelling, the CO had been on the radio handset, urgently asking the patrols if they could see the source of the incoming fire so we could radio for counter fire. The RTO had been seated next to him holding the radio when a piece of shrapnel had flown between them, cutting both the cord of the phone and the throat of the RTO, who had bled out quickly.

We stayed on that ground one more night. The following day, before we moved out, there was one more unusual experience. We had two choppers come in with tourists. These were some of the crewmembers from the B-52 unit that had bombed this area. The Air Force brass must have thought it would motivate those who dropped the bombs to see the effect their weapons had on the ground. I remember just sitting by the side of my hole, watching them stroll around sightseeing, and thinking it was all a bit silly. Those guys could have no idea of the hell on earth those on the ground went through when their 500- and 750-pound bombs were hitting.

I had just experienced the effect of mere 105mm artillery shells. The 500-pound bombs they dropped had a much greater explosive impact, but there was no evidence that their bombs had done much more than uproot trees. It all contributed to the feeling that our military had tremendous power but no idea of how to direct it, or at least not in a direction that made any sense.

The more I thought about it, the tourism angle wasn't what really bothered me about those guys. It was the language the aviators used to describe their work. They don't obliterate people or bomb them senseless; no, they just "deliver ordnance." We in the infantry didn't deliver ordnance. We killed people. I lost respect for those who refused to embrace the reality of their slaughter. It wasn't that I doubted their courage as warriors; I would much rather be on the ground dodging bullets than in the air dodging antiaircraft fire and surface-to-air missiles. I wasn't proud of killing people, but I wouldn't turn away from the reality of it. It seemed to me that somehow we robbed those we killed of their human value when we embroidered the words used to describe the act of ending their lives.

War is about killing, and I had trouble with those who wouldn't acknowledge that directly. At the same time, if one is to cling to any sense of morality, the killing has to be necessary. It has to involve defending yourself; your buddies; and, implicitly, the country that had put you in the field. The cumulative effect of my months in combat and seeing what we were doing in Vietnam was that I began to question the necessity of this war and the killing. I am certain my feelings reflected those of many of the grunts I lived with, as they often approached me with the same doubts and questions about the validity of our participation in Vietnam. I had no ready answer.

Today, we have taken long-distance killing one step further, removing the pilots from the killing machines, whether they are Tomahawks missiles or missile-carrying drones steered from twelve thousand miles away. It raises the question: does killing go beyond self-defense when it's so impersonal, so distant, so easy?

May 1967

The number of American military:

KIA was 443

WIA was 8,380

DOC was 147

CHAPTER 20
CAMP LIFE

We moved that day. We stayed in the Ho Bo Woods area, but we abandoned the bomb craters to set up a battalion fire support base, FSB Martha, several kilometers away. It had been prepared while we spent those few days in the woods. The FSB was in an open area of wild grass and scrub brush on a secondary dirt road, well off the main road to Trang Bang in an area called Sui Cao. There was a small village within sight, a hundred and fifty meters, further north. The FSB had been secured by one of the rifle companies, and our attached battery of 105mm howitzers was sited with us along with the 4.2 inch heavy mortar platoon, the reconnaissance platoon, and the battalion headquarters group. At least it wasn't the muck and water of the Delta area. We had relatively firm ground underneath our feet, which meant we could throw up tents to sleep in with sandbags around them to protect us from mortar or rocket fire. The rifle companies were all out in the field in different camps within a ten-kilometer radius.

We had an incident a day after we moved into the campsite. We had pretty much finished the bunker work, the perimeter wire was in place, and tents had been set up for a few officers to sleep in. We were settling in. The feeling was we would be here for awhile.

I was doing the midnight shift at the battalion TOC, so during the day I just tried to doze on my cot with the tent flaps open to escape the worst of the heat. About 2:00 in the afternoon shots rang out from the side of the perimeter nearest to me. I heard several shots at first, then several more. I grabbed my helmet and M-16, threw on my flak jacket, and ran through the bushes that dotted the inside of the camp. Within seconds, I vaulted over a low bush with my M-16 extended and finger on the trigger, ready to fire. Immediately in front of me stood the battalion commander with his .45 service pistol extended in the air and an angry glare in his eyes. I hit the brakes about five feet from him with my M-16 pointed right at his chest.

He looked at me, surprised that I was on the verge of shooting him. Then he recovered and pointed his pistol around the camp "They're all asleep!" I was speechless. What I was thinking was, "Of course they're all asleep sir. It's after lunch on a hot day in a secure camp in the field." But all I really said was "Yes, sir!" as I lowered my M-16. He continued to complain, "Charlie could hit us now and just walk into camp."

That was it, though I think I got extra points with the colonel for arriving on the scene quickly, ready to do some shooting. I didn't need the extra points though. This was the same CO who had written me up for the Silver Star several months earlier.

Charlie wasn't going to attack us in broad daylight when we could call in artillery and air support that would chew him to pieces. I think the real problem the CO and other battalion commanders had was frustration that this was a squad leader's and platoon leader's war throughout South Vietnam and very much so in our area of operations. We had frequent contact with Charlie, but not on the scale in which the colonel could maneuver his battalion and engage in the large set-piece battle he yearned for so he could be written up as an outstanding combat leader. It was a frustrating war for many mid-level and higher career officers.

* * *

This was in late April. I didn't know it at the time, but this would be my home until the end of my tour a little over four months later. My job would be to help coordinate with the rifle companies in the field and to monitor the TOC radio at night for their reports if they or the patrols they put out were engaged by Charlie.

Though the battalion's rifle companies were operating deeper into the Ho Bo Woods, our FSB was at the edge, just a kilometer or two away from the main road running from Cu Chi north to the town of Trang Bang. Operating at the edge of a fairly well-populated area presented difficulties in distinguishing civilians, who might be innocent farmers, from full or part-time VC. It wasn't an issue deep in the woods; if you saw a guy in black pajamas, he was VC. But, at the base camp, we had many civilians in and around the base throughout the day. There was a collection of farm huts only a hundred meters from the perimeter wire. We occasionally sent out a squad with a translator from the intelligence section (the battalion S2 shop) to question them. Of course, they were all innocent during the day, but the question was would they be digging up their rifles to come at us after dark? Thus, we sent out squad-sized ambush patrols every evening.

My specific duty at that time was supervising the activities in the battalion TOC at night. The patrols were planned during the day and went out of the wire after dark, when I came on duty. I checked the map as to where the patrols had been sent and got activity reports, which most of the time was nothing. The RTO periodically received reports from whatever patrols were out. If there was trouble or contact with Charlie, I got on the radio to offer whatever guidance was necessary. Of course, if it was serious stuff we woke the battalion commander and S3.

I noted one night that we had a patrol set up on the road from Cu Chi to Trang Bang. I was a bit surprised. This was a bit like expecting Charlie to walk down Broadway. At the time we had a 10:00 p.m. curfew in effect. All civilians had to be back home and not moving around after that time. A little after

11:00 p.m. we got a call from the ambush patrol on the road. They had fired on an approaching bus. The bus had stopped in front of them and they were checking it out. I acknowledged their report and asked if they had any wounded or were taking fire. They replied they had no wounded and no incoming fire. I asked about the bus. They said that it was full of civilians with no weapons in sight. I asked about wounded civilians. They said several had minor wounds. The patrol leader asked what they should do. I told them to bandage the wounded civilians up and leave the bus as it was. We would report the incident to the nearest ARVN unit. The patrol should leave the site and retreat to the rally point it had selected for itself on the way out.

A rally point, a spot two or three hundred meters behind the ambush site, was normally selected in the patrol plan. It was to be used when the patrol was engaged and the situation was such that the patrol leader felt his troops needed to back out of the fight or, in cases like this, when the ambush position has been compromised. The patrol leader acknowledged and reported in twenty minutes later, when he had reached the rally point. I told him to set up there and wait out the night.

It was really upsetting. Technically, our patrol was right to shoot. It was after curfew. At the same time, it was really stupid. I didn't blame the soldiers in the patrol. The patrol plan that had set them up on the main road in an area in which there were a lot of civilians made no sense. The captain who had drawn up the plan earlier that day was new to our battalion and had never been in combat. He was just covering what appeared to him to be empty areas on the map, without any sense of the reality of what it looked like on the ground. This tendency of senior officers away from the action to scatter points on the map with marks denoting "boots on the ground" to impress higher commands happened much more frequently than it should have. It was a matter of trying to show the brass how aggressive the unit was under their leadership.

* * *

By this time we had spent several weeks in place, the daily routine of the camp had become fixed and the major battle was against boredom for those of us living all day and all night in the FSB. Our troops were only supposed to leave the wire for operational reasons, and the nearby village was off limits except for our intelligence NCO and his translator, who visited the village chief periodically to gauge the local reaction to our presence and see if they could pick up any useful intelligence. For all that, the drive of the everyday soldier should never be underestimated.

One day, when once again I was unable to sleep due to the heat, I heard someone exclaiming loudly, "My God! Will you look at this!" I got up and walked over to where the noise was and once again found our battalion CO stirred up. This time he had a different interest and was using his binoculars. He was focused on the high grass about seventy meters out from the wire, about halfway to the village. He looked over at me, laughing, and said, "They're doing it in the grass." Apparently one of the girls from the village had walked halfway to camp and signaled to the troopers on line that she was interested in having company and engaging in commercial transactions. We had no watchtowers; each unit manning the bunkers was responsible for observing its own sector of the perimeter. An enterprising and surely horny young soldier had told his buddies to cover for him while he went out to meet the lady to take part in what in Vietnam was termed "Boom, boom." The colonel, on his regular post-lunch walk, had discovered them because he was able to see the soldiers posterior raising and falling in the grass. I left the colonel to his activity and went back to my cot. I don't know what punishment the soldier received, but I'm sure he thought it was worth it.

There were commanders in Vietnam who, in similar situations, had worked out an arrangement with the local population in which the unit's soldiers would have access to an area in which to meet the girls, and the privilege would be rotated amongst the troops based on doing their jobs well. When a unit was stuck in place for an extended period, these arrangements were great morale boosters. The problem was that the top commanders in Saigon, who took care of their own morale boosting in a more convenient fashion, frowned on these "field-expedient" arrangements, as the army termed any such impromptu fixes to issues that were not highlighted in field manuals.

Not all the incidents that occurred were that funny. During our first weeks in the battalion fire support base in the Ho Bo Woods, there was a steady process of digging in by all the troops. This meant, for the most part stringing, barbed wire around the perimeter, filling sandbags, and ensuring that all positions inside the wire were protected by them. Just sitting there, we presumed, sooner or later Charlie would find us a good target for mortar fire, but as each day went by without any action the inevitable happened and we all slowly relaxed.

The explosion, when it came, nearly shook me out of my bunk. It was loud, it was very close, and it got my attention. We were being mortared. It was after midnight and my shift in the TOC had ended more an hour earlier. I was sleeping on a cot in a tent near the TOC which had a sandbag wall around it.

I grabbed my steel pot and M-16, put on my flak jacket, and stumbled out the front of my tent, anticipating more shelling and possibly even a follow-up ground attack. There were no more explosions.

There was shouting from a nearby tent and acrid smoke from the explosion was in the air around it. Someone inside was calling for a medic, and as I walked over one came running toward the tent just as a soldier stumbled out into the open. The flaps were open, and inside I could see a cot had been thrown over by the explosion. An officer we'll call Lieutenant David, the headquarters company executive officer, was lying on the ground moaning in pain. It hit me then that we weren't undergoing a mortar attack. Lieutenant David had been fragged.

The medic who was working on him turned to me and yelled that we needed a medevac right away. I ran over to the TOC and told the officer on duty what had happened, that we weren't under fire but needed to radio down to Cu Chi to get a medevac up to us ASAP. Then I returned to the tent to see how David was doing.

He was still alive and moaning. A small group that had gathered outside the tent was talking about the fragging while the first medic, who had been joined by a second, worked on the lieutenant. Apparently, the man I saw stumbling out of the tent was Lieutenant David's RTO, who had been sleeping in the same tent but on a cot further from the explosion. He was pretty much spared except for some shock and small shrapnel wounds in his arm. Another medic was leading him away to the medical tent to clean him up and bandage his arm.

Apparently, the reason the lieutenant was still alive was that he had folded his flak jacket beneath his head and shoulders as a pillow, and was sleeping in the cot on top of his semi-inflated air mattress and several blankets. Whoever had thrown the grenade had snuck up the side of the tent, lifted the edge, and rolled it into the tent beneath the lieutenant's bunk. Luckily, the flak jacket had absorbed most of the blast. Nonetheless David had sustained severe shrapnel wounds beginning a couple of inches below his armpits and on down his back and legs. The medic's concern was damage to organs such as the liver.

The Department of Defense didn't keep accurate statistics on the instances of fragging during the Vietnam War, and actually there weren't many in its early stages. By the end of the campaign for U.S. combat forces in 1972, when most combat units had been withdrawn, fragging had become a well-reported phenomenon, but in 1967 it was still virtually unknown. The practice became much more common in later years, with numbers reported to be in the range of three hundred to four hundred annually, and rising each year from 1969 to 1971, as soldiers grew progressively unhappy and antagonistic when asked to fight a war that was increasingly unpopular back home.

The medevac chopper landed thirty minutes later. After it had lifted Lieutenant David out of the fire support base, several officers and NCOs from the battalion headquarters spent some time discussing what had happened. It was a real shock. To our knowledge, this had never happened in the U.S. Army in Vietnam, let alone in our unit. Why had this happened to David?

One of the NCOs had an opinion. The military provides for a level of non-judicial punishment that can be administered to enlisted men by company-level officers as they see fit. As XO of the headquarters company, David was responsible for overseeing these punishments for all those assigned to the battalion support units. The most common punishment of this type was called an Article 15, after the section of the code of military justice that allowed it. This could be used by the company officer to address cases of insubordination, drunkenness on duty, returning late from a pass, fighting, and a long list of other minor offenses. The officer could bust the enlisted man down a rank, reduce his pay,, or restrict him to some form of camp duty.

This case seemed to involve being drunk on duty. No alcohol was authorized on the fire base, but the troops would occasionally smuggle some in when returning from leave or duty trips to the rear at Cu Chi, where alcohol was available. In this instance, it was known that David had given an Article 15 to an enlisted man in the battalion 4.2inch mortar unit a few days earlier. This man was the suspect. Now you might say this was a pretty stupid act of revenge for the soldier, in that it would be nearly impossible to get away with it, except that once the grenade exploded there was no physical evidence, and if nobody witnessed it he could deny it until hell froze over. With that in mind, we all hit the sack, but I doubt anyone slept well. I sure didn't.

The next morning, a chopper flew in from Cu Chi with military police and a senior warrant officer from the Criminal Investigation Division (CID). After spending a couple of hours going over the site and questioning several soldiers, they isolated the soldier from the 4.2inch mortar unit and handcuffed him. He was loaded onto the chopper, which took him back to Cu Chi for further interrogation.

There was a some black humor in circulation to the effect that, though the soldier hadn't yet admitted he threw the hand grenade, the flight back to Cu Chi could be dangerous, and that he would probably confess before it was over. The joke alluded to the occasional intelligence section practice of interrogating VC prisoners by taking them for a chopper ride and hanging them over the side until they decided to talk. Apparently the CID warrant officer had expressed confidence that he would have a confession by the time he got back to Cu Chi.

Charlie did come after us late in May, but not in the way we expected. The senior NCO in the intelligence section often visited nearby villages with his translator, meeting with village chiefs to try to build trust over time. Sometimes they would coordinate with medical teams from Cu Chi that would conduct what we called a medical civic action program or Medcap, which basically involved a doctor and some medics entering a village, holding a sick call, and treating all those who showed up. While the medical treatment was underway, the intelligence NCO and a translator spoke with as many of the villagers as possible, trying in a soft way to gain intelligence and the trust of the people, as well as disseminating some propaganda concerning our war efforts. These were programs the Vietnamese government should have been undertaking, but it wasn't doing so in any effective manner. For me, over time, this became one of the issues in Vietnam. The U.S. military was interested, as the slogan went, in "winning the hearts and minds" of the people. This sentiment wasn't in any way apparent among the ARVN troops when we operated with them. The government in Saigon seemed to have other priorities.

Early one morning, the soldiers in the bunkers at one point

on the perimeter noted some metal flashing in the sun about fifty meters beyond the wire. Some troops were sent out to see what it was and brought it back with them to the intelligence bunker. It was a piece of sheet metal about five feet long which had been painted on one side with a propaganda message from the VC for the U.S. troops. Some brave soul had crawled up as close as possible to our wire during the night, propped it up so we would see the sun reflect off it in the morning, and snuck away.

The message on the sign was quite simple: "American soldiers, what are you doing in our country? This is our fight for freedom. Please go home to your families." It was simple and to the point. I had to admire the effort, and the reality was that their target audience, the average American soldier, was beginning to think the same thing.

The previous December, when our unit had been stuck in the rice paddy camp on the edge of the Mekong Delta, my platoon had crowded together on the part of the perimeter we had been assigned to, and built crude wooden shacks to be out of the rain and have a dry base to sleep on. Following basic camp maintenance chores every day, we had a lot of time left to sit around and talk. I had been with the platoon long enough and had gained some credit after our fight in the Filhol plantation, so the guys in the platoon were happy to talk to me directly. I had been approached several times by different troopers who asked the same question, "Sir, what are we doing here? These people don't want us here. This isn't our fight."

I had no good answer other than that we were soldiers and had been assigned a job. We had to do it the best we could so we all got back home safely. Not too inspiring, huh? Now, six months later I was beginning more and more to ask myself that very same question the guys in my platoon had asked then, and which the VC had posed to us on their propaganda poster.

***

It must be emphasized that in the early years of the war, the U.S. military's entry into Vietnam wasn't controversial for the American people or for those of us doing the actual fighting. The post-World War II era was one of overwhelming confidence in the U.S. military, accompanied by an overriding fear of the communist threat to democratic governments around the world. The Communist Chinese had taken over China in 1949, and in the early 1950s our troops had fought to stop the Russian- and Chinese-backed attempt to seize South Korea. We had grown up hiding under our desks at school, preparing for the Russian nuclear attack many felt was sure to come. We had seen TV footage of Hungarian freedom fighters taking on Soviet tanks with their bare hands in the 1956 uprising and being slaughtered in their thousands. We had seen Cuba fall to Castro and the communists, and had experienced the tension of the missile crisis in October 1962. We had watched the building of the Berlin Wall and the shooting by communist border guards of those who dared to dash for freedom. There were U.S. military advisory teams working with anti-communist governments in Latin America, and all these activities were accepted as a matter of course by the American people.

Within that historical context, if the government said the security of America was directly threatened by events in far-off Vietnam, the public was primed to believe it. Direct threats comprise the only acceptable grounds for going to war, regardless of the level of intensity of conflict.

The obligation for young men in America to be drafted or to enlist in military service was taken for granted, at least by working-class Americans. Of the four boys in my family, all served in the military. One of my brothers served in the air force, one in the marines, and the other and I were in the army. Military service and the righteousness of our cause were both accepted without demurrer by the overwhelming majority of young Americans in the early 1960s. By 1964, when I entered the service, Vietnam was starting to get more news coverage, but most Americans were still behind our apparent obligation to support a freely elected democratic government against the North Vietnamese communist effort to subvert and absorb South Vietnam.

The introduction of American combat units into Vietnam in response to the somewhat muddled Gulf of Tonkin incident in July 1965, and the subsequent Gulf of Tonkin Resolution by Congress, was the starting point for the American public to start seriously questioning the government. After the 3rd Marine and the 1st Cavalry divisions landed in Vietnam in August 1965, some politicians and some of the public began to sit up and take notice. But even in 1966, as I finished my years of military training and prepared to fly to Vietnam to do my part, it was clear the bulk of the American people still supported the war and viewed the situation in very simplistic terms as a threat to our country. Of course, as the military effort shifted away from pacification and an advisory capacity toward increasingly major engagements, with accompanying American casualties, that support swiftly began to erode.

After the war, reviewing the evolution of my thinking and subsequent disillusionment based on my own direct observations, it seemed to me quite amazing that the men I served with, fellow grunts with no career ambitions, could see what the colonels and generals couldn't or wouldn't see.

The real situation was that we lacked the support of the Vietnamese people throughout the country, and our total war efforts, such as the declaration of free-fire zones, search-and-destroy missions, and aerial spraying of the toxic Agent Orange, only made situation worse. The common sense of the average man on the ground, the grunts I served with, shouldn't be underestimated. When I try to comprehend why the brass couldn't reach this understanding while the enlisted man could, the best I can come up with is that Westmoreland and many of his generals were blinded by their World War II experience. I assume that in their arrogance, they could only think in outdated terms. Marine

Lieutenant General Lewis Walt and the men in his command deserve all the more credit for perceiving the need for an innovative approach and initiating it. Tragically, Walt's superior, Westmoreland, put an end to his non-violent pacification efforts.

In addition, I firmly believe the accompanying curse for the younger field-grade officers was they were blinded by the need to get their promotion tickets punched in this, the only war they had.

In totality, the only reasonable answer to "Why are we here?" is that we shouldn't have been. We should have packed up and gone home. By the time the VC left that propaganda sign for us, I was well along this path of thought, but I hadn't quite arrived at its end.

June 1967

The number of American military:

KIA was 449

WIA was 4,946

DOC was 99

CHAPTER 21
FINAL DECISION

I had one more major decision to make during my tour, but it wasn't until June that the opportunity arose. I returned to the division base camp at Cu Chi to stay overnight prior to taking my R&R leave. We were allowed one week's R&R during the year we were assigned to Vietnam. I had not taken mine because of my hospital stay, and I really thought I had no right to one. Nonetheless, the admin guys in the battalion sent me a note saying I could still take it. I thought, "Why not?" and signed up to go to Japan for five days.

The chopper from our battalion base camp dropped me off at Cu Chi midafternoon. It was up to me to catch a truck ride over to the area assigned to the Manchus for an overnight stay before I flew out the next morning.

While I waited for a truck, I saw some troops running in formation and singing airborne chants. This was unusual for Vietnam; most grunts were too busy trying to do their job and stay alive, so physical fitness training suffered as a result. I asked an officer nearby if he knew what was up. He told me that these guys were trying out for the new volunteer unit that had been started up by division the previous year. That was the Long Range Reconnaissance Patrol, or LRRP (pronounced "lurp"). He explained that the unit's basic mode of operation was six-man patrols that were dropped in far-off sectors of the division's operations area to try to find Charlie over a period of a week or more. If successful, their orders were to report in, go to a pick-up point, and get out. Larger combat units would follow up to actually engage Charlie.

This focused my attention. Maybe this was what I had been looking for. I asked the officer what the requirements were. He told me that combat experience was required, a recommendation from one's current unit, passing a physical fitness test, and six months left on your tour in Vietnam. I knew I could meet all these requirements except the time. When I returned from R&R, I would have less than three months left in my tour, but that wasn't a major issue. I could extend my tour by three months if need be. The army would be happy to oblige me.

I left it for the moment. I had orders for an R&R, and I would let the possibility of volunteering for duty with the LRRP float to the back of my mind while I took advantage of those orders.

The time in Tokyo was great. It allowed me to relax and distracted me from thinking about Vietnam or my place in it. But, I couldn't escape such thoughts on the seven-hour plane ride back to Vietnam. It was more than three months since my last flight from Tokyo to Tan Son Nhut. On that occasion, I had only one thought: get back to my unit, get back to combat, and do my job in order to redeem myself. Many things had changed during the passage of three months.

I had been dissatisfied with the purpose and prosecution of the war in the time that I had been leading my platoon, but I had felt strongly that I had an obligation to put those thoughts aside, lead my men, and do the best job I could. The time spent serving as a staff officer had provided some distance for a wider assessment of the war, and it had only increased my doubts about our purpose and the ineptitude with which our military machine was approaching the campaign. I certainly wasn't alone. As Platoon Sergeant Amado had written to me in January, "This war isn't worth it."

There was another factor at work that I believe most combat veterans will understand. It's about killing. You can only kill so much. I must be clear that I'm not sure how many VC I had personally killed, if any at all. Whenever I had shot at Charlie, for the most part I was only one member of a group of soldiers who were doing so. If Charlie fell down, only maybe was it your shot. I could never state for sure and had never had a one-on-one shootout. Certainly, I was morally responsible for my complete and enthusiastic participation. But you can't go into combat worrying about these things. Your mind has to be clear. Kill or be killed. When our machine-gunner had mowed down the group of VC charging out of a hut to pick up weapons, I had cheered him on with all my being. As the ensuing fire fight with the VC inside the camp reached its crescendo, I was aiming and shooting with conviction. No thoughts, no regrets. Every other time I was on the line and there were bullets coming in, if I had an opportunity to shoot back, there was no hesitation. I aimed to kill and *hoped* to kill.

Now, however, I faced a clear decision. Right or wrong, I had no doubt I could qualify for the LRRP unit, even though the standards were quite high. I had never failed to qualify in my time in the service and had complete confidence that I could do the job. Map reading and compass work were critical skills that brought Ranger training to an unwanted end for many soldiers, but I was completely confident in that phase of work. But, given my doubts about the mere need for this war, could I step up and do more killing—and doesn't killing chip away at your soul bit by bit? The more I pondered this, the more I felt that volunteering for LRRP now would make me kill again in a war I didn't believe in, and ferry me spiritually to a much darker place in my soul. I don't know how many guys went through a similar thought process. It was a choice many didn't have to make, but I can't believe I was the only one to go down this road both intellectually and emotionally.

It was all very clear to me by the time I got back to Cu Chi. I was through with this war. I would do my operations job for the next few months, return to the States, and start life again outside the military. I had once loved my life in the army, and I would have thought of making a career of it, but now, examining the hatchet job I felt the army was doing on itself, I just saw no future in it.

When I was back at the battalion fire support base in the Ho Bo Woods, I was brought up to date on events that had occurred in my absence, and they confirmed my decision. They involved the loss of two very good soldiers and young men.

Warrant Officer Stan was about twenty-one but looked more like fifteen. He stood 5 feet 6 inches tall, and half of that seemed to be the biggest grin ever to come out of Arkansas. I had flown with him in his H-23 observation chopper many times. Like many young pilots, he loved that machine and thought he could do anything with it. Apparently a senior officer had wanted to go down to Saigon for the night and had gotten permission for Stan to fly him to Tan Son Nhut. Like all chopper pilots in Vietnam, Stan flew at tree-top height to avoid the possibility of ground fire. Such flying became a habit, I suppose, and the guys would joke about having branches stuck in the undercarriage when they finally landed back at Cu Chi. On this occasion, the habit caught up with Stan and his passenger.

It was twilight, definitely a period of lowered visibility. On the approach to Tan Son Nhut, Stan failed to see the power lines just outside the air base until it was too late. The skids caught on the power line, the light chopper flipped over, fell onto the ground, and exploded in flames. My only hope was that he was dead from the crash before the flames reached him.

He had showed me his teenage wife's picture once. She was

very young and very cute. Now she was very alone.

The other was a ROTC grad, Lieutenant Lew, the leader of the battalion reconnaissance platoon. He and I had shared the chopper ride out to the Pineapple Patch in March. He was well over six feet tall and had a rangy, athletic build. He wanted to make a career in the army and enthusiastically viewed his reconnaissance platoon as the modern cavalry, charging about on jeeps with rear-mounted machine guns, finding and fixing the enemy for the battalion. Unfortunately, Charlie was very good at staying away from passable roads and remaining underground. I understood Lew was having little success over the months and was becoming frustrated at losing his opportunity to make a mark.

He was on the road, in the lead jeep as always, when they came to a stream. He and his sergeant got out and walked down the dirt road to the water's edge to check on how passable the stream was. He stepped on a mine at the edge of the stream. It blew off his lower leg, and he bled out before a medevac chopper could be brought in. The sergeant, also caught up in the blast, sustained serious wounds, and died with Lew.

I was sick of the waste of lives. From that point on, I did my time in the manner and mindset of any convict, which was how I was beginning to envisage myself. I just counted down the days to the end of my war.

There was a signature song played on the Armed Forces Radio each evening on a program I think was called Music by Twilight. The program made for a change from the usual rock agenda, and the song was a haunting tune called "Clair de Lune." It came on each day about the time the ambush patrols departed through the wire.

Each evening, before going on duty, I sat on sandbag walls next to my hooch, listened to it, and thought one more day is gone. To this day, when I hear "Clair de Lune," I flash back to that setting and think it's time for ambush patrols to leave the wire.

* * *

July and August passed painfully slowly but without major incident. Then September finally came. It was time to make my last trip down to Tan Son Nhut Air Base.

July 1967

The number of American military:

KIA was 458

WIA was 5,471

DOC was 249

August 1967

KIA was 466

WIA was 4,604

DOC was 122

September 1967

KIA was 460

WIA was 6,909

DOC was 119

CHAPTER 22
RIDING HOME WITH THE GUYS

Being able to hitch a ride on a military transport is one of the advantages of military life, but it can be a double-edged sword, because you don't know and can't guess what awaits. I was on my way back to the States and would ordinarily have been given a voucher for a seat on a civilian plane operating under contract to the military. Nevertheless, I had, at my request, been granted what was called a "delay en route" to my new military assignment in the United States. This provided me with written permission to stop in Japan and take leave on my way back, and that meant that I had to hitch rides on any military cargo planes going my way. As we had an ongoing war in the Pacific area, there was no problem getting a ride. There was a tremendous two-way flow of military air traffic from the States to Vietnam and other points in the Pacific.

The first leg of my trip was to be from Tan Son Nhut in Saigon to Yokota Air Base, just outside of Tokyo. This was an easy ride to catch because all planes going back to the States had to stop at Yokota to refuel. I had caught a chopper down to Tan Son Nhut and spent the night in a transient officers' hooch at Camp Alpha. The next morning, I changed uniforms from my jungle fatigues to the short-sleeved khakis the army considered Class A dress for the tropics and, in summertime, Northern

Hemisphere wear. This was mandatory during that period for any soldier traveling on military orders. The idea was to present the best possible image of the U.S. military to the public while traveling through the States. and around the world.

I was a little put out that morning. I'd had a pretty sleepless night, given the excitement and emotion of leaving Vietnam for good and being able to look forward to civilian comforts. In addition, the dispatch office for soldiers seeking military rides—where I had to report in, show my orders, and wait for a flight going my way that had room for me—was located not far from a Quonset building that had some strong and disagreeable odors coming from it. I asked around and learned that this was the Tan Son Nhut mortuary, where they received the bodies of soldiers killed in action and prepared them for the trip back home to be buried. Whether the odors consisted of the chemicals used to prep the bodies or the smell of decomposition that could come so quickly in the tropics, I wasn't sure. But the knowledge of the building's function, combined with the odors, worked badly on my mind. I was very relieved when the officer handling the bookings called out my name and pointed out an air force cargo jet on the ramp, saying that I could ride out and get on that one. It was clearing to Yokota Air Base, and I was to be the only passenger.

When I climbed up the tail ramp to get on the plane I discovered I was not to ride alone. There were six metallic-gray military caskets on board. They had been loaded two caskets side-by-side in a row and fastened down the center aisle of the plane. The crew chief pointed me toward the front and told me I would be alone on the flight, but, of course, I wouldn't. I would be strapped in on a lateral bench seat alongside the two front caskets. These guys were my company, and I was theirs, on their last ride home. The crew chief left me and went forward to his flight station, which was out of my sight. I was left alone with the caskets.

* * *

I am sure the long plane ride home is one of serious introspection for all combat veterans. That would have been the case for me even without the company of these six soldiers. With the caskets in front of me as a focal point, my soul-searching was an extended, powerful, and searing experience. A whole new wound opened up.

I got up during the flight at least twice and walked around the double row of caskets. I put my hands on each casket and paused while I thought about the young man inside and his family, and prayed for each one. I thought about their ages and their home backgrounds. For the most part, soldiers killed in Vietnam were twenty or twenty-one years old, though I was also aware there could be a couple of NCOs of the same age as my squad leader, Sergeant Ray Nixon, who was thirty-six years old. I wondered where their home towns were and if they have girlfriends or wives. How big were their families? I called up the memories of the guys in my platoon and all my friends who had been killed and included them in my thoughts, prayers, and tears.

I don't know what a psychologist would say about sending home a recent combat veteran with these caskets for such an extended period of time, but it was hardly a healing experience. Instead, I felt an anger growing inside of me, and eventually I focused my thoughts on that. I was angry at the loss. Not just the loss of the lives of these men or of my many friends, but angry at the loss of an innocence that could never be recovered. My soul had been scarred and altered and could never be restored. I realized that some things, very important things emotionally, just like Humpty Dumpty, could never be put together again.

As I sat alone in that chilly plane looking at the caskets, I grew to understand the depth of emotional damage I and all combat veterans sustained. I struggled with my emotions and the many jumbled thoughts that went through my mind. It wasn't just the emotional wounds and sense of loss that was the source of my growing anger. It was also the knowledge that had been growing within me almost from my first days in Vietnam, that our leadership, political and military, had failed us in so many ways. Me, my buddies in combat, my brothers in the caskets, had all grown to adulthood in a period of great faith in our government's political leadership on foreign policy issues, as well as faith that our military power was used to defend our nation from foreign threat. We were the children of World War II and had judged the war in Vietnam in that light. Of course, there was no comparison between the threats to America involved in the two wars. The Japanese had directly attacked the United States at Pearl Harbor. In Vietnam, apart from a debatable domino theory, there was no real threat to America.

That knowledge, built up through daily observation for a year, gave birth to a strong feeling of betrayal. We had been used. We had been used as tools of a bankrupt foreign policy dreamed up by the politicians, and as cannon fodder for career military officers to advance in their race toward a star or two on their shoulders. So it was not just a loss of innocence, it was a loss of faith in our leadership and our cause. I was to learn that I wasn't alone. Hundreds of thousands of my combat brothers as well as millions of Americans at home would come to share that loss of faith.

The total of war dead from the Vietnam War beggars belief. The communists and their supporters in the North and South may have won their war for independence, but the American military behemoth had extracted a terrible price. The number of American military lives sacrificed totaled at least 58,286 dead, and 153,303 wounded. Other allied forces assisting the South Vietnamese sustained nearly 6,000 dead and 16,000 wounded. ARVN dead totaled 220,000 and 313,000 were wounded.

The losses for the communists, North and South, totaled more than 1,000,000 soldiers according to the Vietnamese government, though U.S. Defense Department sources believe the real number is much lower.

CHAPTER 23
BACK HOME

My return to the States was uneventful. I had caught a military flight to Travis Air Force Base, outside of San Francisco. From there I had to cross over to San Francisco airport to catch commercial flights back to Milwaukee for home leave. While I was waiting for a bus at Travis, a plane landed and stopped about one hundred feet away across the tarmac. A large group of soldiers got out to walk around and take a travel break. They were all dressed in brand new jungle fatigues with the 82nd Airborne patch on the shoulder. I guessed the flight was coming from Fort Bragg, home of the 82nd, and had stopped here to refuel on its way to Yokota Air Force Base in Japan and then on down to Vietnam. As I watched the soldiers, I spotted a lieutenant, most probably their platoon leader, talking to them about the guidelines for taking the break. The thought that came to mind was the eternal old soldier's epithet for new troops going into battle: fresh meat. I considered walking over and talking to the lieutenant. He would see the Combat Infantry Badge and the other ribbons on my uniform, and would very probably be open to talking if he felt I had advice for him. On the other hand, what could I say that would be of any use? I decided not to approach him. There was really nothing I could say. I felt deeply sad and sorry for him and his green troops. Many of them would never see their homes again. That was a fact.

When I entered the airport in San Francisco I was holding a rifle bag containing a Chinese copy of the Russian Mossin-Nagant carbine. We had captured it from a VC down in the Delta the previous autumn. No one questioned my carrying the carbine along. There was no security check at the airport, and even when I boarded the plane and showed the stewardess what I was carrying, she didn't blink. She just said they would hold it up front for me and I could pick it up when we landed.

It was still early enough in the war for me not to encounter any resistance as I walked in public in my uniform. Although there certainly wasn't any display of warmth or support, the abuse heaped on returning veterans in later years wasn't evident yet.

My strongest impression was the lack of urgency and awareness I encountered in everyday America. I had just come from the battle zone and was conscious every day and night that our American boys were fighting and dying in the jungles of Vietnam. I was overwhelmed by the normalcy and sedate pace of life in the States. Didn't these people know there was a war on? Didn't they care?

Well, of course they knew, but they had more important things to worry about in their everyday lives. As one returning soldier put it later, "They're more worried about whether they have enough anti-freeze in their cars for the coming winter." I found that reality very depressing. Clearly, the troops in Vietnam were at war, but the American people weren't. Those of us in military service in the combat zone were a world apart and far removed from the daily concerns of America, where life was going on without us. The nation was not at war.

I made my plane connections and arrived home to a warm welcome from my family. I started to get on with life.

My return to civilian life was difficult. All the symptoms that are publicized today as post-traumatic stress disorder (PTSD) were my close companions, though there was no talk of such issues in those days. I was to learn later that these reactions to combat are cited as far back as the 8th century BC Greek classic *The Iliad*, though somehow America seemed to have no idea of such a phenomenon at the time of postwar Vietnam.

The following years were difficult for America and tough transition years for me. I had trouble sleeping, and there were bad dreams about my war experiences. I developed a very short temper. Somehow, with the support of my family, I managed to cope and find my way through further schooling and onward to find a job, but those were tough years.

When you initially emerge from a combat background into the civilian world and find yourself interviewing for jobs, you discover that you have an attitude, a chip on your shoulder. It's a knee-jerk reaction, not something I'm proud of. But you hate finding yourself in a position where, as many vets angrily say, "You have to explain yourself to fucking civilians." I once had a job counselor look at my resume and wonder about "all that army stuff." At the same time I was thinking, "You asshole, I've done things you couldn't approach or even dream of, and you're telling me I don't measure up?" Of course the reality is that job recruiters or advisors know that there are hundreds of applicants for a position, and most positions have detailed requirements other than being able to set an ambush or call in artillery support.

Even so, I think all of us combat vets have this attitude, even if we don't voice it, and I believe people we work or associate with can feel something. It's difficult to define, but the residual impression is adverse. I have no well-defined thoughts about it, either; I wouldn't know how to adjust it, but it has hit me over time that it is real and that it is probably negative. That's just the way it is.

Although I thought the war in Vietnam was a complete, incompetent disaster, I initially had trouble with people being against it, as I felt they were undermining the troops who were still there. Eventually, I came to understand that the best way to support the troops was to get them the hell out of Vietnam, and I came to support the anti-war efforts. In May 1970, when the army invaded Cambodia on Nixon's orders and several young protesters were killed by Ohio National Guard troops at Kent State University, I was outraged. I made the most dramatic protest I could think of. I boxed my medals from my military service and sent them back to the Pentagon with a cover letter protesting the expansion of the war to Cambodia. I sent copies of that letter to my senators and congressman, and I wrote further personal letters to them as well.

For me, that was the conclusion of the war. The protest in America was so strong it was clear that the nation's days in Vietnam were numbered. Our combat units were pulled out in 1971. The 25th Infantry Division was one of the last divisions withdrawn and the one that had sustained the highest number of casualties.

When Saigon fell to the NVA on April 30, 1975, I felt sad for the ARVN soldiers left behind in Vietnam, and I mourned the waste of so many lives because American politicians and military leaders felt they had the right to play God.

I thought the fall of Saigon definitely marked the end of my war and my time in Vietnam. But I was wrong.

Two to three million Vietnamese refugees fled Vietnam during the late 1970s and the 1980s.

According to the United Nations High Commission for Refugees, between 200,000 and 400,000 Vietnamese boat people died at sea.

CHAPTER 24
KEEPING MY WORD

Nearly thirty years after I returned home I was to find that my time in Vietnam wasn't over. In 1994, I accepted a job with an American firm that had an office in Hong Kong. I was to help negotiate their investments in mainland China. I had studied Mandarin, both written and spoken, in graduate school and had traveled and worked in China in the mid-eighties for the U.S. China Trade Council in Washington. D.C., and I had some other skills and background that fit the job. Work and life in Hong Kong and mainland China was an utterly time-consuming and exhausting cycle. Thus, when the Chinese lunar new year rolled around in early 1995, I was happy to have a week or so off to slow down and reflect. It was then that I decided to revisit Vietnam. I didn't really want to go there. The main purpose of the trip for my wife and myself was to tour Thailand.

I still had the three-by-five card Captain Luong Dinh Chi had given me in the hospital in 1966. Despite my reluctance to visit Saigon, I felt I had to keep my promise to Chi to not forget him and his family.

The landing at Tan Son Nhut Airport and entry to immigration was a voyage back through time. None of the major buildings had changed. The airport presented a forlorn picture, drab in its emptiness and lack of upkeep. There was no appreciable air traffic apart from our plane. The Vietnamese Air Force had placed old MiG fighter jets in the same simple open-ended hangars that had housed the American and South Vietnamese fighter jets and air-support aircraft, but there was no activity. It could have been an air museum. It was early February, still the cool season, so the 80-degree temperature was comfortable. The entry building was the same structure through which civilian travelers had passed more than thirty years earlier, but was now very dilapidated. Also, this was no longer the entry point to Saigon, but rather to Ho Chi Minh City, as the victors from the north had renamed it. I've stuck with the name Saigon until today and have found that many of the Vietnamese I deal with in the city also prefer to use the former name.

The biggest change was the absence of bustling foot traffic and the limited presence of soldiers with guns. The terminal was largely deserted and the staff were all dressed in drab olive green Vietnamese military uniforms and caps with red stars on the front. I felt a surge of animosity well up within me. I would have happily shot any one of the bastards. As I studied the government officials who sized me up, I felt the same antagonism on their part, whether real or not. The processing of documents was all done by hand and slow to the point of torture. The air reeked of suspicion. "What are these foreign visitors up to?" seemed to be the main question in the bureaucrats' minds.

Outside the terminal was a crowd of taxi drivers—*not* an organized queue—all yelling for our attention. It was a mob scene and smacked of desperation as the many drivers fought over the small number of arriving passengers. Luckily, we had arranged with the hotel to send a car to pick us up. The ride into town and arrival at the hotel showed a bit of promise, though twenty years after the end of the war the city and countryside lacked signs of any real economic progress. As with China before the leadership of Deng Xiao Ping in the eighties, communist political and economic policy had strangled the possibility of real growth. The streets looked far from prosperous and there was minimal new construction. On the other hand, the streets were busy and signs of commerce, albeit on a basic level, were everywhere. The Chinese new year was just getting underway. Tet, as it is called in Vietnam, is the major holiday of the year. There was a festive aura to the decorations and activities along the road.

The hotel was new, a Taiwanese investment, and while it didn't have the Hong Kong flash we were used to, it would have fit right into the scene in the more established Chinese cities of Beijing, Shanghai, and Guangzhou, to which I often traveled. I began to relax, but after we had checked in the staff put me back on edge by warning us that it wasn't safe to travel around at night because of pickpockets and purse-snatchers. They advised us to check with them before we ventured anywhere outside the hotel. We decided to have dinner there and forego looking around Saigon at night. I knew nothing about the town as I had never made it there during my tour in Vietnam. On this trip, except for fulfilling my promise to Captain Chi, I had no desire to engage in tourism, either in the city or in the country as a whole. Given the dour reception we had experienced at the airport, it seemed the Vietnamese government still wasn't sure whether it wanted tourists or not. If it did, the word hadn't gotten down to the low-level officials who met with foreign visitors.

Morning gave us a new perspective as the clear sunshine and relatively cool air of the season provided a lift to our spirits. I checked with the hotel desk, to show one of the clerks the house address on the card Chi had given me in 1966. It seemed that it wouldn't be difficult to find and would be less than fifteen minutes ride by cyclo, a three-wheeled pedal-powered taxi. My optimism grew. My wife, May, and I set out, but we suffered a setback almost immediately.

We took a cyclo from the rank in front of the hotel because the driver spoke some English. I learned that he had been a captain in the ARVN and he told us that former ARVN soldiers and government officials were not cleared by the communist authorities for any meaningful work. Thus, even twenty years on, virtually all of the cyclo drivers were former ARVN soldiers. This taxi work, essentially the bottom step of the economic ladder, was all they were allowed.

This was the first indicator to me of how completely the communist police state apparatus controlled the lives of everyday people. We would encounter this aspect of life in post-war Vietnam again and again throughout this and subsequent trips.

The driver pulled up on a street lined with shop houses, the normal style of living for many small merchants, with a shop on the ground floor and family living quarters on the second and third floors. The driver indicated that Chi's address wasn't on the street itself. He pointed down a narrow alleyway on which similar houses were crowded in side-by-side. He said he would wait for us. I told him it might take an hour or more, but he said it was okay, he would still wait. I understood: times were tough and he needed the assured money that our ride back to the hotel offered.

May and I walked down the lane looking for the right house number, which we found after only a few paces. The interior wooden door was open, but there was a closed iron outer grille through which we could see inside. I heard voices in an unseen room and knocked on the door. At first there was silence, then more talking before a young man in his early twenties came to the door. His eyes widened in surprise at seeing two westerners standing there.

I held up the card I had been given by Chi and asked if this was the home of Captain Luong Dinh Chi. For a second, the young man was speechless. Then he shouted something in Vietnamese into the other room and a lady in her late fifties emerged. I repeated my question, again holding up the card with the house address and Captain Chi's note.

The succeeding few minutes were pandemonium. The iron door was thrown open and the lady grabbed me by the hand and told me to come in. The house was filled with a babble of

Vietnamese, everyone talking at once. The lady pulled me to a chair at a table in the second room, never letting go of my hand, and indicated that we should sit down. All the while, she shouted instructions to the two young men in the house to fetch us drinks and food. She was smiling and crying at the same time.

After all these years, I had found Chi's home and family.

We heard some of the story over the next hour. We were too late for Chi. He had died of cancer in July 1988. I learned that this lady was his wife and that he had eleven children who survived him. Most of them were out of the house, trying to make a living. Those present in the house had very limited English-language ability.

Chi's wife, who I came to address simply as "mother", as her children did, asked us to come back in the late afternoon, when most of the family would be present for the traditional new year's dinner, and a daughter who spoke good English would be there to translate. May and I promised to return. So she would be reassured that we would indeed return, I gave Chi's wife my business card, together with the card for the hotel where we were staying. We left and went back to the hotel while trying to absorb all that had happened and wondering what more was in store for us.

When we returned at four in the afternoon, there were at least eight of Chi's children present, including Doris, the daughter who spoke English and could translate for us. They had arranged for her to speak with us for thirty minutes before dinner to provide all the details of their story.

Doris brought out a picture book and led us to another room, where she sat on a sofa, alone with May and me, and started at the beginning, the days of the fall of Saigon in 1975.

Chi had been promoted to major and fought against the communists right up to the final days of the war, at his duty post commanding a tiger commando unit in Vung Tau. The press of his duties was such that he had not been able to return home since 1974. Though Saigon fell to the troops from the

North on April 30, 1975, the family had already experienced the war directly when a mortar shell fired by the communist forces forging into the city hit the roof of their home on April 26. None of the family was injured. Doris showed us the shrapnel damage in some of the rooms.

Some days before the fall of Saigon, the family had received a letter from Chi, delivered by a soldier in his unit, in which he told them that he expected to be captured soon by the communists. He asked his wife to look after their children. They knew little else. Some days after the fall of Saigon, Viet Cong cadres from Vung Tau, arrived at their home. The mother told them, "You already have him." The communist capture team were aware of this and, for whatever reasons, possibly to see if former ARVN soldiers came looking for Chi, decided to move in with the family. They stayed more than a month.

The family told me one aspect of Chi's capture earlier was related to them by Chi's military driver months later. The driver in reality was an underground Viet Cong who told them he had received orders near the end of the war to assassinate Chi. He didn't do it because as he told the family, he knew Chi was an "honest and good man and had a good family" even if he was the enemy.

Chi knew the political military group within the Viet Cong had him marked based on his position as a political commando group leader; they would definitely be hunting him. The communists had carefully prepared lists of those they had singled out for special attention. Chi had been fighting against them too long and too hard to escape their attention. Moreover, he was originally from the North, one of the many Catholic refugees who had fled to the South in 1954. The communist leaders involved in the massacre in Hue in 1968 had admitted targeting Catholics as "particular enemies of ours." Chi's position was similar to that of many of the Vietnamese mid-level officers. These men lacked the resources to arrange an escape that would include their families. Many of the top-ranked ARVN generals had the funds to make such arrangements, and the rank to ensure they could utilize U.S. and ARVN military ships and aircraft. Chi was a man of great moral strength and sense of duty. He stayed at his post and fought to the end.

Chi was not to be back with his family until November 1987. For more than twelve and a half years, he journeyed through the gulag of labor and political re-education camps called *hoc tap* in Vietnamese. Unfortunately, the concentration camp guards didn't reflect the understanding that his Viet Cong driver had demonstrated. Chi was subject to hard labor, constant beatings, and a starvation diet day after day, year after year. His family told me that all the hard labor was done at night. I thought this might be done to possibly minimize public awareness of the treatment of these men. His wife, after finally learning of his initial place of imprisonment, had been able to visit every three months or so, and to leave some packages of food for him. Whether or not he received the food depended on the mood of the guards.

The papers provided by the government at his discharge showed he had been shifted around among nine different camps in all. The final three camps were in North Vietnam, near Hanoi. These camps were reserved for those prisoners whom the communists felt had not repented of their fight against them. The family said that Chi told them later he had probably been marked for shipment to the northern camps due to a defiant remark he made to the guards at one camp about Ho Chi Minh's having a mistress. This story of Ho Chi Minh's mistresses, while generally accepted as being true, even in North Vietnam, is highly taboo among the communist leadership, who make exaltation of Ho Chi Minh a centerpoint of their politics, saying that Ho was "married to the country." Chi must have known he was sure to be punished for it. It shows the indomitable spirit of the man, that he would fight back in this way even after years of imprisonment and abuse.

Doris shared with us two photos of her father. One photo

was taken after his promotion to major; it showed him sitting at his desk, a stalwart, solidly-built soldier, staring straight into the camera. The second photo was of Chi lying in his bed in the family home after the communists released him in November 1987. He is smiling in this picture, I presume that was due to his joy at being reunited with his family. But the smile was incongruous. He also looked as frail, as skeletal in his appearance as a Nazi concentration camp survivor. His body was covered in tumors and bruises. Doris told me the family had done their best to nurse him back to health, but he had died of cancer the following July. The contrast between the two pictures was shocking. Chi's appearance in the second photo was heartbreaking. He was an honest soldier, not one of Saigon's legion of greedy generals and politicians. They had all managed to arrange escapes with their savings and their families to Southern California. Chi deserved better treatment then the vindictive abuse handed out by his captors.

The situation actually got worse for the family after Chi's return and death. At the time, the United Nations had negotiated with the Vietnamese government an arrangement, set up with the U.S. State Department, called the Orderly Departure Program (ODP). The concept involved the Vietnamese government allowing the emigration to the U.S. of former ARVN soldiers and their families. The U.S. State Department would handle the paperwork, which required that the ARVN soldier apply on behalf of his family and list his service in the war against North Vietnam. For Chi's family, this was the only hope for economic and political salvation.

As the family of an ARVN officer, they were, as was our cyclo driver, banned from education and not allowed access to any meaningful work. They had just been scraping along, trying every available form of street work. A prime job had been to go down to the docks in the early morning hours, when the fishing boats came in, buy the fish wholesale, and then retail them on foot throughout the city. This was arduous work, and little profit was to be made as so many others were trying to do the same. Chi's oldest children were now in their early thirties and educated, but they could not be accepted for any meaningful job as the necessary permits from the local communist neighborhood watch authorities would not be granted to them.

Doris told us that she and her older sister had tried to escape by boat years earlier, but they had been caught out at sea by the communist authorities. All those on board had been brought back and put into a re-education camp for six months. Her older sister refused to give up, and a year later had successfully gotten out by sea and made her way to a refugee camp in Singapore. There was talk of pirates intercepting the boat and hardships suffered prior to an international cargo vessel picking them up, but Doris gave no details. I was hesitant to push, having heard many horror stories of the atrocities visited on Vietnamese refugees by Thai and Malay pirates in the South China Sea. After several years, the older sister had finally found her way to America, where she was then resident.

The older sister and Doris were the family's two rays of hope. The family expected that the older sister would be able, through the immigration process, to achieve American citizenship and then start the business of bringing Mother over to join her. That of course would be many, many years in the future, if ever. Doris, who had been eight years old when her father was taken away, had somehow learned cooking skills as well as English, and was employed as an assistant or demi-chef in the kitchen of a foreign-owned hotel.

Chi's wife was overjoyed when she learned of the ODP. This meant the entire family might be able to go to the United States together. She had obtained the paperwork, and with Doris's help, filled it out and provided the documentation of Chi's service in the ARVN, his imprisonment, and death. This had been done two years earlier. Many months after the application was submitted, she was shocked to learn that it had been turned down. The reason, reflecting the beautiful logic of the bureaucrat, was that the form had to be submitted and signed by the person who had served in the South Vietnamese military, not his family. Of course, Chi was dead thanks to his imprisonment and abuse by the communists he had fought against, so he couldn't apply, and thus the family was ineligible. Instead, they were condemned to continue living at the base margin of economic survival in Saigon for the foreseeable future.

That was the outlook when I knocked on the door.

Now, with the celebratory air in the room and their constant comments to one another and May me that they felt I represented their father's return from the spirit world to help them, it was painfully obvious that the family regarded me both as their hope and as their father in spirit. They said that of all the Americans Chi had served with during the war, I was the only one who had contacted them.

After dinner, when we returned to our hotel, we talked over the situation. May was adamant about making the very good point that "it would be a terrible thing to get their hopes up that you can help them, and then not be able to deliver." I agreed, but my riposte was that, no matter what, I had an obligation to try.

The next day, before traveling on to Thailand, I met with the family and told them that I could make no promises, but that I would do my best to help.

Sources have estimated that 165,000 South Vietnamese died in the re-education camps out of one to two and a half million who were sent there.

CHAPTER 25
FIGHTING THE PAPER BATTLE

It was definitely the most unusual interview in which I had ever taken part. When I entered the office at midday, the lights were out and the curtains on the window pulled shut. The only illumination filtered around the edges of the curtains. It was a twilight setting. My eyes soon became accustomed to the gloom, and I saw my host sitting behind his desk on the left of the room as I entered. He waved me to a chair in front of his desk, and then gestured for me to be quiet by holding up a hand and putting a finger in front of his mouth. He pointed to another desk at right angles to his, backed up almost to the wall. There was a chair there, but it was empty. He whispered, "It's my assistant, Duc. He was an NVA tank driver during the war and had malaria. He's not strong and needs to nap a couple of times during the day." Then, looking underneath the desk, I could see there was a slight figure curled up on the floor. I just nodded as if this was an everyday thing, turned back to Andre, and held up a hand to signify understanding and compliance. This was the time that Andre had told me to stop by his office, so I asked if it was still okay to have our talk. He said, of course; we just had to speak at a lower volume.

Andre is Jean Andre Sauvageot, a retired U.S. Army colonel and, at the time of this meeting in his office in Hanoi, the representative of the General Electric Company in Vietnam. I had met Andre during the early 1980s, when he worked for the Northrop Corporation at an office in Rosslyn, Virginia. At the time, I ran my own marketing consulting firm, Asia Investor Services, and was there to discuss a possible contract with Northrop for research work in Asia. Andre's specific area of expertise was Vietnam, but he was effectively functioning as a Southeast Asia regional consultant to Northrop. The firm had two research contracts to let, one for Indonesia and a second for Japan. My firm was subsequently able to win the contract to provide industry research on Japan.

Andre and I had a good conversation that day in 1984; it turned out we were both Vietnam veterans. His background was much more extensive than mine, though. He had originally gone to Vietnam in 1964 as a major hoping to serve as an advisor to an ARVN ranger battalion. Instead, he ended up serving at the provincial level, advising on the training and deployment of the Vietnamese government's regional and provincial forces. Andre picked up the Vietnamese language, and proved to be so fluent that he continued to serve almost throughout the war in a variety of roles in what some analysts call the "other war," the civil development and pacification effort that went under many names. Andre's commitment to the other war was such that, though he carried a .45-caliber sidearm, he let the Vietnamese he worked with know he would never use it. In essence, the pacification effort was doomed to failure from the beginning, due to the base corruption of the Vietnamese government and the antipathy of the American general staff, which favored World War II-style large-unit engagements over such a soft other-war approach. Much of the South was already lost by 1964, as the communists had successfully appealed to the peasant population that was ignored by the government in Saigon.

I had kept in touch with Andre occasionally over the years. Previously, I had heard that he had been stationed at the American Embassy in Bangkok working with the ODP. Now I learned that he had come to Hanoi several years earlier to open an office for GE. Attempting to find the most effective way to assist Chi's family, I thought Andre could be a source of advice and assistance.

Andre's advice was to the point and very helpful. First, a matter of great importance to me, he gave me hope that I could manage the bureaucratic requirements to get a review of the rejection Chi's family had received. He gave me the ODP office contact in Bangkok and said my recommendation, based on personal contact with Chi, would make a difference. At the same time, he warned me that the program had been in operation for more than ten years already and was being brought to an end, so I had best move quickly.

His second suggestion to give weight to my request was to search out other possible supporters, American soldiers who had served with Chi, and get them to write in the family's behalf.

Back at work in Hong Kong, I thought about how best to proceed. I did have some strengths on which to build a case for Chi's family. For a start, I had served in the U.S. Foreign Service as my first job out of graduate school. Though my area of responsibility was economic work, I had been exposed, as had all junior officers, to the "book", the large volume of regulations that govern consular work in the embassies overseas. This is a forbidding labyrinth of regulations that is constantly being updated as new situations arise around the world. One thing I had learned about the State Department is that it is an organization extremely sensitive to congressional inquiry. I decided on a two-prong approach. First, I would write directly to the Bangkok office of the Orderly Departure Program and make my strongest possible case to them, based on my own service record and direct knowledge of Chi's service, and I would describe my meetings with the family and its desperate situation. Second, I would write to my U.S. congressman and senators, including any others, such as Senator John McCain, who might be sympathetic, and ask them to inquire of the State Department if it would be possible to review the rejection of Chi's family. In addition, through contacts gained from a Vietnamese refugee friend who was active in the community in Arlington, Virginia, I was able to post notices in veterans' publications, asking for anyone who had served with Chi to contact me and help with the campaign to bring his wife and children to America. Several ex-soldiers replied to me and promised to help with the writing campaign. This process took more than a year, and I visited Chi's family in Saigon twice to reassure them that I hadn't forgotten them, that I continued to fight to have their case reviewed.

We had some success relatively quickly with the application for Chi's wife to come to the U.S. She was granted a visa in early 1996. The problem, however, was that the U.S. regulations, as they were constituted at the time, would not allow children over twenty-one to accompany the mother. As more than twenty years had passed since the end of the war and Chi's imprisonment, all of his children were over the age limit.

The effort turned into a campaign, carried out by many parties besides myself, to get Congress to change the regulations to allow unmarried children of any age to emigrate. By May 1997, a year and a half later, I had a stack of documents and correspondence on the case that was a foot high.

Then we were rewarded. I received a letter from the program saying the family should reapply and that they would review the case. It took some months more, but we subsequently received a notice that Chi's children had been accepted and would emigrate to the United States to join their mom and the eldest daughter living in northern Virginia. Eight of Chi's children, led by Doris, arrived in the States on August 11, 1998. Doris told me years later that, while on the plane coming to the U.S., she had a dream in which her father's spirit was on the plane with her, standing next to his children and smiling with joy.

The family endured an extremely difficult time after it relocated to the U.S. Many of the support programs put in place to assist Vietnamese refugees during the immediate post-war years had expired. But the family has worked hard and is doing well.

All of the younger generation have sought schooling and are employed at worthwhile jobs, and most are now American citizens. Doris has married and she and her husband Russ are raising a teenage daughter, Vi, who is doing very well at school.

I visit them periodically, but I must admit that I sometimes find it difficult. When the family members look at me, especially Mother, they seem to see Chi's spirit looking after them. I continue to wish them well and try to keep in touch, but that is a lot to carry. I was just keeping my word, one soldier to another.

Helping Chi's family was a final chapter in my war, and I'm grateful that I had the opportunity and ability to do it. But it doesn't excuse my failure. I wasn't where I was meant to be on February 26, 1967. In my heart, I have always understood that was where I was supposed to be, and where I was intended to die, and I really can't forgive myself for that failure. At the same time, I'm sure I'm not the only soldier who has such thoughts and carries such hidden wounds. I have had to do what we all have to do: pull ourselves together and get on with a responsible, giving life, because that is the best way to honor those we left behind.

AFTERWORD

One of the reasons I hesitated so long to write this book, besides the personal pain it caused me, was that I was unsure as to the value of my experiences. I used to feel the storytelling should be left to the real war heroes rather than just an ordinary soldier trying to do his duty, succeeding at times and failing at others. But in the wake of events in Iraq and Afghanistan, I am increasingly convinced that many of my thoughts and insights are still valid today. The people I served with were special and deserve to be remembered. I certainly wasn't a hero (except of course in my family's eyes!), but I owe it to them to tell these stories.

I mentioned earlier that, some years after the war, I was privileged to meet and become a friend of a real hero, Dave Hackworth, a soldier who was legend to junior infantry officers in Vietnam and the author of *About Face*. This is the story of his military journey, starting at the age of seventeen in post-war Europe, and going through both the Korean and Vietnam wars to become the most decorated living American soldier before his death from cancer in 2005. Hack didn't speak of heroes, but the highest compliment he could pay an infantry soldier was to call him a "warrior". Hack was certainly a great American warrior.

But, as much as I admire Hack and the other men I wrote of before, Audie Murphy and Ross S. Carter, it occurs to me that their stories are atypical, indeed the stuff of legend, but that my stories are really much more representative of the typical grunt—the average young man who went to war and made the best of it. Those average guys include the soldiers with whom I served. These are men who went the extra mile on a daily grind-it-out basis but received few awards. To borrow a phrase now used by CNN, these soldiers were "everyday heroes." These were not men who looked for military glory or career advancement. Rather they simply sought to serve their country and do their duty to the best of their ability.

This definition includes men like one of my squad leaders, Sergeant Bobby Wood, the young skier from New York who joined the army asking to be assigned to the winter soldiers, the 9th Infantry Regiment, then in Alaska, but found himself traveling along with the 9th Infantry to Hawaii, and then on to Vietnam as the U.S. army mobilized. It was Sergeant Wood who warned me not to take the end seat in the Huey chopper that flew us to my first combat LZ. Bobby was then shot while sitting in that same seat during an airmobile assault months later, because he wouldn't allow any of the soldiers in the squad he was leading to sit in the most dangerous position. The list includes another of my squad leaders, Sergeant Ray Nixon, a skinny man, only 5 foot 6 inches tall, who spoke to me of walking through rice paddies as a soldier in Korea in 1952, and then wondered what the hell he was doing walking through rice paddies again in Vietnam in 1966. Sergeant Nixon died after getting out of his foxhole during the most intense phase of the February 26 battle, running to the rear for ammunition for his troops. On his return he was killed by the enemy after exposing himself to their fire in a heroic manner. I'm sure he would have said he was just doing his job. It includes Spec 4 Bob Carnoske, my RTO, who once showed me his favorite picture from home in St. Louis, a 1957 Chevy, clean and beautiful. He was promoted to a presumably safer position as the company commander's RTO, only to be killed when the VC made assaulting the command post a key part of the attack on the company position. When two squads of my platoon and I were locked in the fire fight in the Filhol Rubber Plantation in which I was wounded, all of these men and Sergeant Amado, my platoon sergeant, volunteered to join the relief force that came out in the dark of night to help us. One of the motivations I had to write this book was the fact that many of those who fought this war have passed away over the years. My stalwart platoon sergeant, Frances K. Amado, retired from the army, moved from Hawaii, and worked as a security guard in Las Vegas. He passed away in 2006.

If I knew their names, the list would include the six young men whom I accompanied on one leg of their last ride home. I sat with them in the cargo plane taking us up to Yokota Air Force Base in Japan.

There are many more. I keep their names and go over them and think of them often, and I will do so until I die, wishing I had been a better soldier while serving with them.

I respect the superheroes and the "special" soldiers of all types. I acknowledge that they were and are invaluable in our war efforts, but the truth for me is that it is the average guys, the simple grunts, the everyday heroes doing much more than average things on a daily basis who win our wars for us. This book is for all of those who served in World War II, Korea, Vietnam, Iraq, Afghanistan, or any of our wars or "incidents". God bless them and keep them.

One of Alpha Company's soldiers was awarded the Medal of Honor for his actions during the February 26, 1967, battle. That was First Sergeant Maximo Yabes. His citation reads as follows:

YABES, MAXIMO

Rank and organization: First Sergeant, U.S. Army, Company A, 4th Battalion, 9th Infantry, 25th Infantry Division.
Place and date: Near Phu Hoa Dong, Republic of Vietnam, 26 February 1967.
Entered service at: Eugene, Oregon. Born: 29 January 1932, Lodi, Calif.

Citation: For conspicuous gallantry and intrepidity at the risk of his life above and beyond the call of duty. 1st Sgt. Yabes distinguished himself with Company A, which was providing security for a land clearing operation. Early in the morning the company suddenly came under intense automatic weapons and mortar fire followed by a battalion sized assault from 3 sides. Penetrating the defensive perimeter the enemy advanced on the company command post bunker. The command post received increasingly heavy fire and was in danger of being overwhelmed. When several enemy grenades landed within the command post, 1st Sgt. Yabes shouted a warning and used his body as a shield to protect others in the bunker. Although painfully wounded by numerous grenade fragments, and despite the vicious enemy fire on the bunker, he remained there to provide covering fire and enable the others in the command group to relocate. When the command group had reached a new position, 1st Sgt. Yabes moved through a withering hail of enemy fire to another bunker 50 meters away. There he secured a grenade launcher from a fallen comrade and fired point blank into the attacking Viet Cong stopping further penetration of the perimeter. Noting 2 wounded men helpless in the fire swept area, he moved them to a safer position where they could be given medical treatment. He resumed his accurate and effective fire killing several enemy soldiers and forcing others to withdraw from the vicinity of the command post. As the battle continued, he observed an enemy machinegun within the perimeter which threatened the whole position. On his own, he dashed across the exposed area, assaulted the machinegun, killed the crew, destroyed the weapon, and fell mortally wounded. 1st Sgt. Yabes' valiant and selfless actions saved the lives of many of his fellow soldiers and inspired his comrades to effectively repel the enemy assault. His indomitable fighting spirit, extraordinary courage and intrepidity at the cost of his life are in the highest military traditions and reflect great credit upon himself and the Armed Forces of his country.

***

Men I knew of my 2nd platoon who also died that day were:

Ovie Earcil Blankenship, E-3, age 20, Cincinnati, Ohio
Harry Philip Brightman, E-3, age 24, Louisville, Kentucky
Larry R. Butcher, E-4, age 20, Pecks Mill, West Virginia
Robert Thomas Carnoske, E-3, age 22, St. Louis, Missouri
Bradley Chavis, E-4, age 21, Pembroke, North Carolina
Ray Nixon, E-5, age 36, Tacoma, Washington
Richard Tomasini, E-3, age 19, San Francisco, California

Additional Alpha Company casualties:

Vincent Junior Cannizzaro, E-3, age 20, New York, New York
Theodore H. Davis, E-6, age 32, Neshaminy, Pennsylvania
Robert Leon Harvey, E-4, age 19, Moore, Oklahoma
Lynn Elmo Hunter, E-5, age 22, Ogden, Utah
Allen Harvey Katz, E-3, age 26, Santa Monica, California
Donald Eugene Madden, E-3, age 19, New River, Tennessee
Hugh John McCormack, E-4, age 22, New York, New York
Arthur Alan Niedermeier, E-3, age 21, Newark, New Jersey
Matthew Theodore Orton, E-3, age 23, Gideon, Missouri
Wayne Keith Sippey, E-3, age 19, Pittsburgh, Pennsylvania
Jack Riley Trim, E-3, age 24, Southhaven, Mississippi

BIBLIOGRAPHY

There have been an endless number of books written about America's disastrous intervention in Vietnam. Like many veterans who were caught up in our country's greatest failure of the twentieth century, I have read many of them. Here I specify a few that I used for background on different aspects of my experience:

Bao Ninh, The Sorrow of War: A Novel of North Vietnam 1990
Carter, Ross S., Those Devils in Baggy Pants Appleton Century Crofts, 1951
Hackworth, David, About Face: The Odyssey of an American Warrior Touchstone, 1990
Hastings, Michael, The Operators Phoenix, 2013
Herr, Michael, Dispatches Knopf, 1977
Junger, Sebastian, War Grand Central Publishing, 2010
Krakauer, Jon, Where Men Win Glory: The Odyssey of Pat Tillman Doubleday, 2009
Milam, Ron, Not a Gentleman's War Texas Tech University, 2009
Murphy, Audie, To Hell and Back Henry Holt & Company, 1949
Oberdorfer, Don "Hue Red Report Found," Milwaukee Sentinel, December 6, 1969
Race, Jeffery, War Comes to Long An: Revolutionary Conflict in a Vietnamese Province University of California Press, 1972
Shay, Jonathan, Achilles in Vietnam: Combat Trauma and the Undoing of Character Scribner, 1994
Terzani, Tiziano, Saigon 1975: Three Days and Three Months White Lotus, 1997

Walt, Lewis, Strange War, Strange Strategy: A General's Report on Vietnam Funk & Wagnall's, 1970

Amongst web sources used were:

Amervets.com—a source for U.S. military Vietnam casualty statistics.
G2mil.com—a source for casualties in the Ho Bo Woods.
Manchu.org—this is a site put up by the 4th Battalion 9th Infantry Regiment, veterans that provides a memorial to the regiment's KIAs in Vietnam and extensive background information.
Wikipedia is the source for Vietnam War casualties, both communist and non-communist, as well as background on fragging.

TOM CROWLEY'S origins are in the American Midwest town of Milwaukee. His education was at Marquette University and the John Hopkins University School of International Studies (SAIS) in Washington DC. His career has spanned service in the U.S. Army as an infantry rifle platoon leader serving in combat in Vietnam where he was wounded and awarded medals for valor. It was exposure to Japan, during a period of medical treatment that led to his fascination with Asia. After returning to the U.S. to complete his education he joined the U.S. State Department as a Foreign Service Officer specializing in economic analysis of Asian countries. He subsequently joined the General Electric company of the U.S. to become the first country manager in Korea. He continued working with GE and other power generation and investment firms, living in almost every country in Asia for a twenty-five year period until the Asian financial crash in 1997.

Living in Thailand at the time of the crash he decided to explore a different path in life and volunteered at the Mercy Centre, a Bangkok based NGO working to provide education to the poorest slum children, provide shelter for street children and treatment for children and adults with HIV/AIDS. Tom has continued with programs assisting street kids to this time. His writing reflects his varied experiences living and working in Asia. He is a member of the Mystery Writers of America and the Military Writers Society of America. He divides his time between a home in Kensington, Maryland in the U.S. and Bangkok.

Tom's first book, *Bangkok Pool Blues*, was non-fiction and grew out of his fascination with the game of pool. He can be found in his leisure time in Bangkok competing in and, every once in a while, winning local tournaments. His primary writing interest however is in creating good action/adventure fiction built around the character of Matt Chance, an ex US Army ranger wounded in action and retired in Bangkok. Tom enjoys the writing of both Connellys, Michael and John, Elmore Leonard, and Stephen Hunter amongst others.

Crossing the Chicken
A Jake Diamond Mystery
J.L. Abramo

Down & Out Books
September 2019
978-1-64396-030-2

Vinnie "Strings" has been double-crossed, shot and left for dead at a crime scene, and framed as chief suspect in the murder of an influential businessmen.

Jake Diamond has a strong dislike of the *double-cross*. If asked why the chicken crossed the road, Jake would suggest the road had *crossed the chicken*. Jake frantically scrambles to find answers before the case is closed with Vinnie taking the fall.

The Dead Beat Scroll
An August Riordan Mystery
Mark Coggins

Down & Out Books
September 2019
978-1-64396-031-9

Private investigator August Riordan's quest to avenge the death of his old partner drops him in the missing person case his partner was working when he died.

An alluring young woman named Angelina is looking for her half-sister, but what Riordan finds instead is a murderous polyamorous family intent on claiming a previously unknown manuscript from dead Beat writer Jack Kerouac.

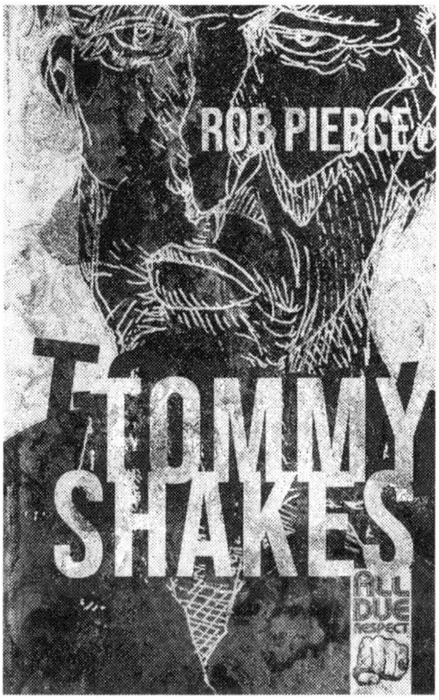

Tommy Shakes
Rob Pierce

All Due Respect, an imprint of
Down & Out Books
September 2019
978-1-64396-034-0

Tommy Shakes is a career criminal, and not a very good one. He earned his name as a heroin addict. He's in a marriage he wants to salvage. He convinces himself that his wife will stay with him if he can bring home enough money. She tells him that won't do it, but Tommy gets a crack at a big heist and decides to pull the job.

The job is ripping off a popular restaurant that runs an illegal sports book in back. A lot of money gets paid out on football Sundays; the plan is to pull the robbery on Saturday night. What can go wrong?

Chasing China White
Allan Leverone

Shotgun Honey, an imprint of
Down & Out Books
September 2019
978-1-64396-029-6

When heroin junkie Derek Weaver runs up an insurmountable debt with his dealer, he's forced to commit a home invasion to wipe the slate clean.

Things go sideways and Derek soon finds himself a multiple murderer in the middle of a hostage situation.

With seemingly no way out, he may discover the key to redemption lies in facing down long-ignored demons.

Printed in Poland
by Amazon Fulfillment
Poland Sp. z o.o., Wrocław

50769844R00153